"Then Osborne
Said to Rozier..."

"Then **Osborne** Said to **Rozier**..."

The Best Nebraska Cornhuskers Stories Ever Told

Steve Richardson

TRIUMPH
B O O K S

Triumph Books and colophon are registered trademarks of Random House, Inc.

Library of Congress Cataloging-in-Publication Data

Richardson, Steve.
  Then Osborne said to Rozier: the best Nebraska Cornhuskers stories ever told / Steve Richardson.
       p. cm.
  Includes bibliographical references.
  ISBN-13: 978-1-57243-999-3
  ISBN-10: 1-57243-999-8
  1. University of Nebraska–Lincoln–Football–History. 2. Nebraska Cornhuskers (Football team)–History. I. Title. II. Title: Best Nebraska Cornhuskers stories ever told.
  GV958.U53R53 2008
  796.332'6309782293–dc22

                                        2008006206

This book is available in quantity at special discounts for your group or organization. For further information, contact:

Triumph Books
542 South Dearborn Street
Suite 750
Chicago, Illinois 60605
(312) 939-3330
Fax (312) 663-3557

Printed in U.S.A.
ISBN: 978-1-57243-999-3
Design by Patricia Frey
Editorial Production by Prologue Publishing Services, LLC

Photo Credits:
All photos courtesy of University of Nebraska unless otherwise indicated.

This book is dedicated to all the people I worked with in the old Big 8 Conference office in Kansas City and also the Sports Information staff at Nebraska. At Nebraska, Don "Fox" Bryant, Bill Bennett, Chris Anderson, Tom Simon, Becky French, Keith Mann, Will Rudd, and a host of others have been great over the years. Nebraska home games were always an event. And Fox always rolled out the Big Red carpet for visiting reporters, as have Chris and Keith in later years.

At the Big 8, DeLoss Dodds, Steve Hatchell, Butch Henry, Mike Scott, Johnny Overby, John Erickson, Helen Atterbury, Jeff Bollig, Ed Grom, Bill Hancock, Tim Allen, Tracie Dittemore, Linda Shetina Logan, Richard Martin, Julie Dorn McBride, Carl James, Tom Starr, Dru Hancock, Prentice Gautt, Becky French, Jeff Seal, Chuck Neinas, Carrollyn Miller, D'Anne Carnahan, Tammy Gannon Byler, and Bruce Finlayson were among the working cast for a conference that epitomized the highest levels of competition and integrity in college athletics. Starting in the early 1970s, the Big 8 Conference office was located in the penthouse suite at the River Hills Mark I Building in downtown Kansas City at Eighth and Cherry, overlooking the nearby Missouri River. The Big 8 office operated in those cramped quarters before moving to a larger location in the nearby Kansas City garment district before becoming the Big 12 and leaving Kansas City altogether for Dallas in the mid-1990s.

table of
contents

acknowledgments

Having grown up in Big 8 country while a student at the University of Missouri, I always had a fascination with Nebraska football. The Cornhuskers rolled out good football teams with precision for more than 40 years, from the early 1960s through the early part of this century.

As a college student in the early 1970s, I only got to see the tail end of the Bob Devaney era at Nebraska. But I was fortunate to be sitting in the stands at his last game against Notre Dame in the 1973 Orange Bowl.

Over the years, I have followed Nebraska through my coverage in the news media, first with the *Kansas City Star*, later with the *Dallas Morning News*, and for the last 11 years as executive director of the Football Writers Association of America (FWAA). Over the years, numerous assistants, including strength czar Boyd Epley, players, and coach Tom Osborne were of great help in covering those teams, along with other Nebraska players and the Cornhusker Sports Information staff headed by Don Bryant and later Chris Anderson and then Keith Mann.

In the last decade or so, my association with the Outland Trophy (which the FWAA presents to the best interior lineman in college football) has brought even more insight into the Nebraska program. Special thanks go to all the former Outland winners from Nebraska, especially to Aaron Taylor, the most recent winner in 1997. He has given of his time generously. And another tip of the hat goes to Bob Mancuso of the Greater Omaha Sports Committee, who also has shared his insights.

Participating in lengthy interviews for this book were Adrian Fiala, Turner Gill, Jim Walden, Aaron Taylor, Mike Rozier, Frank Solich, Eric Crouch, Kris Brown, Ahman Green, Mike Minter, and Barry Alvarez. These people spanned several different eras as players, assistants, and head coaches. Opposing players and coaches such as Pat Jones, Dean Blevins, Jim Dickey, Lynn Dickey, Mike Price, Darrell Ray Dickey, Eddy Whitley, Duke Revard, T.J. Leon, Tom Stephenson, Sam Adams, and others provided great opinions. And administrators such as Bill Byrne, Steve Pederson, Steve Hatchell, Wayne Duke, Jack Lengyel, and Dick Tamburo were also helpful over the years. FWAA members Mike Griffith and Gene Duffey helped gather some interviews for this book.

Thanks to all.

Dallas, 2008

prologue

As a reporter first for the *Kansas City Star* and later at the *Dallas Morning News*, Nebraska football brings back a lot of fond memories of watching some of the best teams in college football over nearly a 40-year period. Cornhusker Red also conjures up some not-so-fond ones. The first two times I actually observed Missouri-Nebraska games, the Cornhuskers beat my Tigers by a combined score of 98–0; 36–0 in 1971 and 62–0 in 1972.

When I was a student at Missouri (from 1971 to 1975), and for years before and afterward, the Nebraska game was always the biggest game of the year, bar none. Sorry, Kansas. Tigers fans aspired to beat the best, and sometimes ended up losing to the less-than-mediocre Jayhawks. Maybe Jim Leavitt, the current South Florida head coach who starred in MU's defensive backfield from 1974 to 1977, put it best this past summer when asked about the Nebraska rivalry.

"Nebraska, I like to beat them because they were the best," Leavitt said. "Personally, I wanted to beat Kansas, and I grew to hate Kansas because we were supposed to. But it was never as big a game as Nebraska was. I thought guys were cocky at Nebraska, and I wanted to beat them." Missouri did it twice while Leavitt was at MU, 21–10 in 1974 and 34–24 in 1976. Both times in Lincoln.

During a 1975 ABC national telecast of Nebraska's 30–7 victory over Missouri in Columbia, a Missouri coed at Harpo's summed up what her life at Missouri was all about. Forget studying: "We just live for football weekends." Unfortunately, it was one of those not-so-proud Tiger moments associated with Nebraska football.

There are a lot of images that revolve in the mind about Nebraska football: Misty's, which served the best prime rib in the Midwest, in Lincoln…Beef sandwiches in the previously cramped Nebraska press box, where there seemed to be more people dressed in red than reporters. But the stat service was always great. And the cheering was muffled…Watching Johnny Rodgers personally taking apart Notre Dame in the 1973 Orange Bowl...Friday night press parties at the Legion Hall in Lincoln, where a certain former coach named Bob Devaney would hold court...Don "Fox" Bryant turning pale when coach Tom Osborne went for a two-point conversion during a game at Kansas in the 1980s, with Nebraska leading by more than 30 in the first half...Kansas State kicker Steve Willis on the sideline at Nebraska's Memorial Stadium during a lopsided loss to Nebraska in the early 1980s: "I knew this was going to be a bad game when our team bus got stopped on Friday for speeding on the way to Lincoln," Willis said.

And then there's Kansas State sports information director Glen Stone's comment to the late Virgil Parker of the Lincoln newspaper. Virgil was known to write mostly favorable stories about his beloved Cornhuskers. When Parker asked Stone if there would be a golf cart to pick him up in the press parking area, which was a football field or two away, Stone responded, "Yes, Virgil, your rickshaw will be waiting."

I also remember Osborne's numerous press conferences—conducted in monotones. Osborne's answers were boring and as consistent as Nebraska's belting of Kansas and Kansas State from the late 1960s through the next 30 years. Osborne was the preacher, and he had quite the flock.

Nebraska fans would increase the populations of Lawrence and Manhattan in the 1970s, 1980s, and in Lawrence in the 1990s, by 15,000 or 20,000 people each Saturday the Big Red played in those towns. And in the mid-1980s as Missouri football went in the doldrums, the same occurred in Columbia for several years.

"I loved them when they came to Columbia, they would buy 15,000 tickets in the end zone, they'd buy every ticket," said Jack Lengyel, who was at Missouri in the 1980s, first as an associate athletics director and then as athletics director. "When we went up there, we had our little group of 250 wearing black and gold."

The 1997 Missouri-Nebraska game in Columbia was one of the all-time classics, won by the Cornhuskers 45–38 in overtime.

The kicked ball in the end zone, which wound up as the Cornhuskers' reception that tied the score, is well documented here.

The following summer, my good friend, *Omaha World-Herald* columnist Tom Shatel, another Missouri graduate, was in Dallas covering a Nebraska game against Texas. I offered to take him and his wife, Jen, to brunch on Sunday. Jen opted for a sports bar for NFL football. That was no problem with Tom, more beer there. I was Tom's best man when they got married. At the end of the reception toast, I mentioned as a joke that Missouri really won the 1997 game. I was booed by the crowd of 500 in the ballroom at the Doubletree Hotel in downtown Omaha. Wrong move. It was a reminder to me, you don't ever joke about Nebraska football, particularly when the bridesmaids are wearing red for a summer wedding and have husbands who look like they could play on the line for Nebraska.

introduction

Nebraska football had its beginnings in 1890.

Faculty member Dr. Langdon Frothingham, a Harvard graduate, led the Cornhuskers to a 2–0 record and even broke his leg scrimmaging with the Nebraska team, which shut out the Omaha YMCA and Doane College.

Through 1910 Nebraska had a series of 10 other coaches, including the legendary Fielding H. Yost, who in 1898 led Nebraska to an 8–3 record before becoming head coach at Kansas in 1899 and later winning a national title at Michigan in 1901.

In 1911 coach Jumbo Stiehm led one of the most successful coaching runs in Missouri Valley Conference (MVC) history when he directed Nebraska to five straight league titles from 1911 to 1915 and most of a 34-game unbeaten streak. He also doubled as the school's basketball coach but left for Indiana after the 1915 season because of a salary dispute. His 91.3 percent winning percentage (35–2–3) is still the best in school history.

Nebraska was the early MVC power, winning or tying for nine of the first 11 titles. In 1914 and 1915 Nebraska laid claim to two national titles. Stiehm's 1915 team beat Notre Dame 20–19, handing the Irish their only loss of the season.

In 1921, after a two-year MVC suspension for violation of league rules, the Cornhuskers won three MVC titles in succession under coach Fred Dawson. Nebraska's 11-game series with powerhouse Notre Dame through 1925 proved to be highly competitive and drew attention to the program. Nebraska moved into the big-time of college football in 1923 with the opening of Memorial Stadium, which drew 30,000 fans for a game against the Fighting Irish that season.

Nebraska produced two later-to-be-recognized consensus NCAA All-Americans during that era, end Guy Chamberlin in 1915 and tackle Ed Weir in 1924 and 1925, before moving into the Big 6 Conference in 1928.

While the rest of the country suffered through the Great Depression, Nebraska football flourished during the early and mid-1930s under coach Dana X. Bible, who had been hired away from Texas A&M. In eight years, Bible, who also served as the NU athletics director for five years, and Nebraska won six Big 6 titles and compiled a 50–15–7 record before Bible was lured by more money to the University of Texas after the 1936 season.

From 1928, when the Big 6 was formed with six members (Nebraska, Oklahoma, Iowa State, Missouri, Kansas, and Kansas State), through 1940, Nebraska won nine league titles.

But the 1940s brought the start of a more-than-20-year drought in league football championships following the 1940 Nebraska team's Big 6 title and first bowl game in school history, the Rose Bowl. Nebraska, under Biff Jones, lost to Stanford 21–13 in Pasadena that season. After the 1941 season, Jones was called to serve his country and never coached football at Nebraska again.

The Cornhuskers went through seven coaches, 22 seasons, and a generation of students and fans, before they won another league football title in 1963.

A major reason for Nebraska's downfall in football in the 1940s was the fact the Lincoln, Nebraska, campus did not have a naval training program during World War II, which would have attracted a pool of top athletes. They wound up enrolling and playing for other schools and against Nebraska. Put at that disadvantage, Nebraska suffered nine straight losing seasons from 1941 to 1949. The previous lack of military personnel on campus lingered even after the war was over. Once Nebraska started losing, it fell from the national spotlight, couldn't recruit well outside of what was already a non-populous state, and posted just three winning seasons in the 1950s.

In 1954 Nebraska did go to the Orange Bowl under coach Bill Glassford as the second-place finisher behind Oklahoma in the Big 7 Conference. The league had a no-repeat rule, and the powerful Sooners had played in Miami the previous season. But the Cornhuskers' lopsided 34–7 loss to Duke in the Orange Bowl was impetus for the Big 7 to abolish its no-repeat edict.

The other Cornhuskers high point of the decade came in 1959, when a 4–6 Nebraska team upset coach Bud Wilkinson's Oklahoma juggernaut 25–21 in Lincoln. That ended the Sooners' 74-game unbeaten streak in league play. The Sooners had not lost a league game since the 1946 season, with an incredible record of 72–0–2 during that span.

The first Nebraska games I remember watching were in the mid-1960s, when the Cornhuskers had a two-year dip and Devaney's teams finished with 6–4 records in 1967 and 1968. The Nebraska-Oklahoma game, by that time, had become an ABC-Television staple on Thanksgiving Day or the weekend after and was a game to look forward to after the turkey dinner. More often than not, the game would determine the Big 8 champion through the mid-1990s, before the Big 12 was formed and the teams quit playing on an annual basis in the league's two-division format. A 47–0 Thanksgiving loss to Oklahoma in 1968 was a low point for Devaney before Nebraska climbed to national championship heights.

The first Nebraska game I saw in person was Missouri-Nebraska in the fall of 1971. I was a freshman at Mizzou. The Missouri-Nebraska series had been extremely competitive in previous seasons. This season it would not be. Nebraska's team would go on to win a second straight national championship after beating Oklahoma in the Game of the Century and then thumping Alabama in the Orange Bowl.

On a clear, sunny day in Columbia, the powerful Cornhuskers–behind Jerry Tagge, Jeff Kinney, and the incomparable Johnny Rodgers on offense–carved up a 1–10 Missouri team, 36–0. On defense, Larry Jacobson and Rich Glover toyed with MU's rather anemic offense in Al Onofrio's first season as head coach. I will never forget, there was one guy in our dorm who was a Nebraska fan. He wasn't from Nebraska–he was just a Nebraska fan. He always had a transistor radio glued to his hip on Saturdays with a piece in his ear listening to his Cornhuskers football game broadcast. He wore a red letter jacket to class with an "N" on it. And in 1971 he was the happiest guy on

Missouri's campus every Saturday while the Tigers were usually losing.

Spared the next season from having to observe in person a 62–0 drubbing of Missouri in Lincoln, I did catch up with the Cornhuskers in Miami, watching them crush Notre Dame 40–6 under the lights in the Orange Bowl. It was Rodgers's personal highlight film and Devaney's final game as head coach in a grand setting. Little wonder Nebraska won. Using the comparable score philosophy, the week after Missouri was bombed by 62 points by Nebraska, the Tigers walked into South Bend as more-than-five-touchdown underdogs and upset the Fighting Irish 30–26.

I saw Tom Osborne's first defeat as Nebraska's head coach, 13–12, in Columbia in 1973. And again the next season, a 21–10 upset by Missouri in Lincoln, the first of three straight MU victories over Nebraska on Nebraska soil.

But there were plenty of other games along the way that did not involve Missouri. As a reporter first for the *Kansas City Star* (from 1976 to 1987) and then for the *Dallas Morning News* (from 1987 to 1996), I was at some college stadium most Saturdays in the fall. And as executive director of the Football Writers Association of America since 1996, I still see several games a year in person involving college teams.

In Kansas City I not only covered Missouri but Kansas and Kansas State. And those teams were always Big 8 fodder for the powerful Cornhuskers. I never did see KU or Kansas State beat the Cornhuskers during my coverage days. The biggest excitement for those games was usually seeing if you could make kickoff because of the game-day traffic caused by Big Red fans.

To that end, the difference between this book and others on the Cornhuskers, is that this will allow for perspectives from those outside of the Cornhuskers family.

From the early 1960s through the end of the millennium, Nebraska's program was one of the most successful in college football. During that period, two coaches basically provided the continuity, with a core of assistants; a walk-on and weight program provided the solidarity or bedrock; and a galaxy of star recruits from New Jersey to California provided the offensive punch and the speed on defense to compete for the national title most years. A long line of quarterbacks, I-backs, fullbacks, and grinding offensive linemen made Nebraska's offense one of the truly fearsome machines of college football for four decades.

Watching Nebraska play without Turner Gill on the field in 1981 against Penn State, the Cornhuskers lost 30–24 to Penn State in Lincoln to fall to 1–2. The next game, Gill played against Auburn, became a fixture at quarterback, and Nebraska was off to a great three-year run. In 1983, Gill's senior season, his two-point conversion pass went astray, or the Cornhuskers would have completed a rally to beat Miami in the Orange Bowl. They lost 31–30 in one of the great finishes of any college football game in any era. For more than a decade, Osborne had to live with the fact he gained respect nationally for not going for the tie, but probably lost the national title in the process. A tie probably would have kept Nebraska number one in the final polls, considering they were playing the Hurricanes on their home field in the Orange Bowl.

Osborne won his first national title in 1994 with a perfect season, 13–0, rallying against nemesis Miami in the Orange Bowl again to edge out another unbeaten, Penn State, which beat Oregon in the Rose Bowl. It was finally his redemption on the big stage and forever eliminated the tag he couldn't win the big one. He had etched his name alongside Devaney's in Huskers lore.

A few months later, I remember the 1995 Nebraska opener on a Thursday night on ESPN against Oklahoma State. Getting an unusual perspective with a seat close to the field, one could determine the size and speed of this Nebraska team. Deep, fast, and physical, the Cornhuskers would have no equal that season, and, aside from the 1971 title team, might be considered Nebraska's best team ever. A 62–24 victory over number-two Florida in the Fiesta Bowl capped a 12–0 season. To show the depth of this team, Ahman Green was a freshman running back and on third team!

Coupled with 13–0 1994 and 12–0 1995 seasons, Nebraska entered the first season of Big 12 competition in 1996 with a 25-game winning streak.

In the second game of that 1996 season, I watched stunned as most people did at Sun Devil Stadium as Arizona State shut down Nebraska 19–0 to end the streak. Before the game, the Arizona State president predicted a Sun Devils victory. And Arizona State's fast-charging defense, led by end Derrick Rodgers, did just that.

Several hours later, defending national champion Nebraska's 26-game winning streak and number-one ranking were history.

Still, Nebraska didn't lose another game during the 1996 regular season, had risen back up to a number-three ranking, and had a chance at a third straight national title. But Texas upset the Cornhuskers 37–27 in the first Big 12 title game. Otherwise, Nebraska might have won an incredible four straight national titles—something no team has ever done.

In 1997 they finished 13–0, won a share of the national title (Coaches Poll, No.1), and Osborne retired after 25 years as head coach.

A standard of excellence started by Devaney had endured under his assistant coach, Osborne. In Osborne's final five seasons, the Cornhuskers were 60–3, from 1993 through 1997. Admirably, Osborne engineered longtime assistant Frank Solich, the former Nebraska fullback under Devaney, as his successor.

The challenges were all of a sudden in the Big 12 Conference where Texas, Texas A&M, and Texas Tech injected speed and talent from the Lone Star State into the mix and provided better competition for Nebraska, which had been the most successful team in the Big Eight along with OU for a 25-year period.

Still, the Solich years resulted in a 75 percent winning percentage, a 58–19 record, one Big 12 title, two north division crowns, and six bowl berths, which carried forward a Nebraska uninterrupted postseason tradition started in 1969 and continued through 2003.

Nevertheless, after the 2003 season Nebraska fired Solich following a 9–3 regular season and before a victory over Michigan State in the Alamo Bowl. NU athletics director Steve Pederson went away from the Nebraska roots and hired Bill Callahan from the Oakland Raiders, who brought in the West Coast offense. He promptly failed to go to a bowl in 2004 with a 5–6 record.

It was Nebraska's first losing season since 1961 (under Bill Jennings, 3–6–1), the year before Devaney arrived as head coach.

The Callahan era was even shorter than the Solich regime, lasting just four years. Pederson, who hired Callahan, was fired midway through the 2007 season after a 45–14 loss to Oklahoma State on homecoming weekend, when the 1997 national title team was honored.

The next week, there was another homecoming of sorts when Osborne was hired as the interim athletics director. He would later fire Callahan and hire LSU assistant Bo Pelini to restore the Nebraska tradition he and Osborne once helped create. And by the way, Osborne's "interim" tag was eliminated.

The team is set to try and bring Nebraska football back to its glory.

chapter 1

Bob Devaney: The Beginning of Nebraska's Dynasty

Nebraska coach Bob Devaney is carried across the Orange Bowl after his Cornhuskers defeated Notre Dame 40–6 on January 1, 1973. From left are: Randy Borg (19), Jerry List (85), Mike Beran (62), and John Kinsel (27).

Before the 1962 season, the Nebraska coaching job went to the wispy, charismatic Irishman named Bob Devaney, who had no links to the Cornhuskers state. But Devaney had an attractive résumé because he had made a winner of a downtrodden Wyoming football program in the western frontier of America after spending his early years in Michigan.

Bob Devaney was a Midwesterner through and through, but not a Nebraskan. He was a football end at Alma College in Michigan in the 1930s, graduating in 1939. During the next decade he was a Michigan high school football coach at such places as Big Beaver, Keego Harbor, and Saginaw before a seven-year stint at Alpena High School (52–9) earned him a spot as an assistant on Biggie Munn's staff at Michigan State.

"Devaney played college football, but he was probably a better baseball player and boxer than he was a football player," said Adrian Fiala, who played at Nebraska from 1967 to 1969. "Being a boxer, that's where his toughness came in….Bob wasn't very big. But he was a kind of a stocky guy. There are some guys you can just kind of look at and say, you don't want to fool with them."

In 1957 Devaney could have wound up as the Missouri head coach. He had been considered for the Missouri post when Don Faurot retired from coaching following the 1956 season and slipped into the Missouri athletics director's chair exclusively.

"At the time, Bob Devaney was going to Wyoming [from Michigan State] and Frank Broyles was an assistant at Georgia Tech under Bobby Dodd," said Dick Tamburo, who was an assistant football coach in those days and later the Missouri athletics director. "Bob called me and asked, 'If I get the Missouri job, will you come as line coach?' Shortly after that, Frank Broyles was named Missouri's head coach."

By the time Devaney took the Nebraska head coaching job, Missouri already was a national power under Dan Devine.

In 1957 Devaney's first Wyoming team was 4–3–3. But in 1958 Devaney took Wyoming to the Sun Bowl, where his

Cowboys beat Hardin-Simmons 14–6. His 1959 Wyoming team (9–1) would have gone to the Gator Bowl if it hadn't been on probation for a recruiting violation.

"That Wyoming team was one of his favorites," said Jim Walden, who was Devaney's quarterback then at Wyoming and later an assistant coach at Nebraska. "It was a catalyst team. It was his first big winning team. They loved him at Wyoming. Bob, keep in mind, spent 14 years in high school football and had been an assistant at Michigan State. He was not some wide-eyed graduate assistant type. He was in his forties when he took the Wyoming job. It was a different environment [in Wyoming].

"The media was, like, the play-by-play guy on the radio, the sports editor of the Cheyenne paper," Walden continued. "The *Laramie Daily Boomerang* had one guy. There was no TV to speak of. A press conference at Laramie was him and a couple of guys going down to the bar and having a beer. Everything was looser and everything more fun. He enjoyed it immensely. And he transferred it to us. He took chances on guys from Wyoming. He had a great staff. I was amazed how much he demanded of you. He wasn't Bear [Bryant] and tried to kill you. But he demanded a lot from you. We maybe were not as good as the players Nebraska had. But we were going to be as good as we could be."

Walden, playing in the Canadian Football League, visited his former coach in 1961 at Wyoming before Devaney took the Nebraska job following that football season.

At Wyoming, Devaney compiled a 35–10–5 record in five seasons and had won or tied for four Skyline Conference titles. His 1960 Wyoming team led the country in total defense (149.6 yards allowed a game). And in 1961 Wyoming finished ranked 17th in the final United Press International Poll.

Devaney had requested and received a new five-year contract. So when he made the decision to leave, he created quite a stir and drew resentment in Wyoming.

"I was sorry to see him leave Wyoming," Walden said. "But I was happy for him. I wasn't sure it was such a great move, looking at Nebraska's record. And he was leaving a good football team....I wished him well and thanked him for him what he had done.

"I could only surmise that any player at Nebraska, brace up, because he will coach you to the bone," Walden continued. "His assistants at Wyoming–John Melton, Carl Selmer, Mike Corgan, and Jim Ross–they understood him and they were a nice team together. If it was any way possible to be good at Nebraska, help was on the way. Coach Devaney was such a good communicator. He would nudge you or pull your aside and said you were not doing enough, and say, 'You can do better.'"

Devaney's First Season

In the early 1960s Nebraska's program was in a state of disrepair and in a 20-year drought. Devaney's predecessor at Nebraska, Bill Jennings, had a 15–34–1 record from 1957 to 1961. He was the seventh straight NU head coach to have an overall losing record at Nebraska since Biff Jones had a winning mark of 28–14–4 from 1937 to 1941.

When Jennings was fired at Nebraska, he made the statement: "There is an intense desire to do something good in this state, like elect a president or gain prominence in politics. But we can't feed the ego of the state of Nebraska with the football team."

Jennings was about as adept at knowing what ultimately would feed Nebraskans' egos as he was at coaching football. Devaney, hand-picked by Nebraska athletics director Tippy Dye, put together a football program that would rise to national prominence, even beyond what he had done in Laramie.

Nebraska hadn't won more than two league games since the 1956 season, but Devaney won five in his first season, and the Cornhuskers, third-place finishers in the Big Eight, became a bowl team in 1962.

Nebraska's only two losses in 1962 were to powerhouse Oklahoma and to Missouri. Guard Bob Brown, Devaney's first All-American at Nebraska, was a star on that team. Warren Powers, later a Nebraska assistant coach (1969 to 1976) and Missouri head coach (1978 to 1984), was a senior defensive back for these Cornhuskers before playing six years for the Oakland Raiders.

Nebraska hadn't even scored on Missouri in the previous four seasons, all under Bill Jennings, losing 10–0, 28–0, 9–0, and 31–0. In 1962 the Cornhuskers at least broke that streak in scoring a touchdown in a 16–7 loss to the Bluebonnet Bowl–bound Tigers. A 34–6 loss to Bud Wilkinson and Oklahoma in the season finale was the one time when Devaney was outfoxed by Wilkinson, who surprisingly unleashed quarterback Monte Deere as a passer. He had three passing touchdowns against Nebraska in Norman.

Immediately, however, Devaney's personality took over the Nebraska program, which had been languishing in a league dominated by Oklahoma in the late 1940s and 1950s under Bud Wilkinson. Oklahoma won 12 straight outright league titles from 1948 to 1959 before Missouri broke the string in 1960. But Nebraska was about to become the next dynasty of the Midlands.

"Devaney was a funny, funny man," said Wayne Duke, who was the commissioner of the Big Eight during much of Devaney's tenure at Nebraska. "He was a carbon copy of Duffy Daugherty. He was on the same staff with Duffy at Michigan State [who was an assistant and then became head coach]. Bob was a humorous guy. He had a lot of jokes....Bob was a lot smarter than he looked. He was always a step ahead, except for Bud, of course. He did not have any sideline comments about Bud. But Bud wasn't there too long while Devaney was coach at Nebraska."

Devaney was not only a tremendous organizer and communicator with his staff and players, he was a great recruiter. And this was obvious from the very beginning. His first recruited class included running back Frank Solich, who later became a Nebraska assistant and then head coach.

"His personality was very easygoing and he was a great recruiter," said Solich, who was from Cleveland, Ohio. "He came into our house. And to be very honest, my father did not want me to leave to go to school. But after Coach Devaney's first visit, they were ready to pack my bags. He just had that charm about him. He came across as a very good guy who you could trust and want to have your son go play for. As a coach, he had the ability get the most out of people."

Once a player was on his football team, he did not became just a number, either, often rare in big-time college football.

"Bob Devaney understood on an individual basis what every played needed as a person, as an individual," Fiala said. "That's pretty rare in a lot of programs where people come and go and they just kind of run them through. Bob knew how to motivate each of us individually. Some guys needed a pat on the back. Other guys needed a kick in the back. Some guys needed just a short discussion. Other guys needed to get chewed out. And Bob knew what each player needed."

It didn't take long for Devaney to register a landmark victory, either. It occurred in his second game when he took his Cornhuskers to Ann Arbor, Michigan, where they beat the Wolverines 25–13. Leading 19–13 in the fourth quarter, the Cornhuskers' pivotal play was a fourth-and-eight conversion inside the Michigan 30 when quarterback Dennis Claridge hit Dick Callahan for a first down to the 16. Bill Thornton's 16-yard touchdown clinched the game.

From the very beginning, Devaney had an even keel about him, mixed with a sense of humor

"A lot of people thought he might come in, in halftime and really lay it down," Fiala said. "Usually at halftime, you are so busy trying to adjust what you are doing offensively and defensively. We would break up into offense and defense right when we came in. With two about minutes left before we would go back on the field, Bob would, if we needed it, he just had a good old sense, an Irish way of how to motivate you....He wouldn't want to embarrass anybody.

"One of the great lines Bob had when Oklahoma was leading us, I was not on the team at the time. The only thing he did at halftime, he came in, and Jerry Tagge tells it pretty well because he was there. He didn't come in until about two minutes before and he poked his head in the door and looked around and said, "Okay, excuse me, ladies, I was looking for my football team." That just fired everybody up."

Devaney's First Nebraska Postseason Trip: Gotham Bowl

One of the most exciting games played at Yankee Stadium was Nebraska's 36–34 victory over Miami in the 1962 Gotham Bowl. But only a crowd of 6,166 showed up at the game, in part because of a shaky promoter, frigid weather, and a newspaper strike in New York City. The bowl folded after the game.

"It was 14 degrees above, and by kickoff it was 9 degrees," said Don Bryant, who was sports editor of the *Lincoln Star* and later the University of Nebraska sports information director. "They played on frozen turf and had to wear tennis shoes. But it was one of the greatest games ever. In the fourth quarter I remember being on the sidelines, and there was a garbage can with a fire in it where the cheerleaders were trying to keep warm.

"Nobody thought there were that many people in the stands. I remember they shut the power off after the game. It was so cold in the press box, we went back to the hotel to file our stories."

The 1960 Gotham Bowl at Yankee Stadium was canceled when an opponent could not be found for Oregon State. Baylor beat Utah State 24–9 in the 1961 Gotham Bowl at the Polo Grounds before 15,123 fans. Finally, the 1962 Gotham Bowl was to be played at Yankee Stadium. But Bryant said the 1962 Gotham Bowl nearly failed to materialize.

"The promoter, Bob Curran, had guaranteed Nebraska a check for $35,000, but Nebraska officials were skeptical that he could pay it," Bryant recalled. "The Nebraska chancellor at the time had the team wait at the airport to take off back in Lincoln, while

Nebraska end Larry Donovan (87) defends a pass play against Miami during the second quarter of the Gotham Bowl at New York's Yankee Stadium on December 15, 1962.

some Nebraska officials and some other sportswriters, already in New York City, took the check to the bank. It bounced. Curran said, 'Give me an hour.' He presented a check that cleared the bank, and the Nebraska team took off."

According to Bryant, Devaney said before the team went on the frozen field before 6,166 fans, "I am sorry I got you into this damn mess. It reminds me of those old back alley fights when I was back in Michigan....There's nobody here to watch, but the toughest son of a bitch will win."

It was a classic game shown tape-delayed on ABC's *Wide World of Sports* and resulted in Nebraska's first bowl victory in history. The Cornhuskers had lost their previous two bowl games to Stanford in the 1941 Rose Bowl and to Duke in the 1955 Orange Bowl. And they nearly dropped to 0–3 in bowl games.

The score was tied 20–20 at halftime, and each team scored two touchdowns in the second half of the game. The difference was Nebraska added two two-point conversions, one by Claridge and the other by running back/guard Bill "Thunder" Thornton while Miami kicked both extra points. The last two-point conversion gave Nebraska a 36–27 lead early in the fourth quarter.

But Miami was far from done. Led by quarterback George Mira, who passed for 321 yards, the Hurricanes sliced the lead to 36–34 with just under 10 minutes remaining. A last-minute interception by the Cornhuskers' Bob Brown of a Mira pass in the end zone saved the game for Nebraska.

Frank Solich was just a freshman and preparing back in Lincoln for the next season during the Gotham Bowl.

"I remember going to the weight room when the team was on the trip to the Gotham Bowl," said running back Solich. "I was trying to get bigger and put some weight on. We didn't have much of a weight room then. It was a pretty lonely deal. There weren't even a lot of guys who lifted weights in that era in 1962. That was over in the old fieldhouse. It was much smaller than the new one they opened up. And it really wasn't organized, not like you see today. It was not a year-round program."

The Growth of Memorial Stadium Under Devaney

Nebraska football was hardly a cash-register ringing affair after World War II and into the 1950s. And it didn't have any major permanent seating increases until shortly after Bob Devaney arrived more than 40 years after the stadium was built.

Memorial Stadium, with 31,000 seats, was opened in 1923 and dedicated in a scoreless 0–0 tie against Kansas.

Nebraska would play before overflow home crowds during the years, but the first actual addition wouldn't occur until 1964, Devaney's third season, when permanent seating was increased to 48,000 after south end zone seats were added to form a horseshoe. Nebraska had gone to the Orange Bowl in the 1963 season after winning its first Big Eight title since 1940 to spur fan interest.

And the 1963 title was also followed by Nebraska titles in 1964 and 1965, Nebraska's first conference three-peat since 1935 through 1937 in the old Big 6. The 1963 through 1965 Big 8 titles led to further increases and eventually the longest sellout streak in major-college football history.

In 1965 Memorial Stadium seating was increased to 53,000 when the center portion of the north end zone was added. And a year later, the completion of the north end zone with both sides brought the capacity to 65,000. It would stay at that capacity until Devaney's final season, 1972 (following back-to-back national championships in 1970 and 1971), when the south end zone was extended by 9,400 seats and the capacity went to nearly 74,000.

In 1962, Devaney's first home game against South Dakota, a 53–0 Nebraska win drew a crowd of 26,953, which would be the lowest home crowd of the Devaney era. In those days school kids could pay a nominal amount, lunch money really, and sit in the "knot hole" section in the end zone.

As Nebraska increased seating, it kept selling out. Nebraska's consecutive home-game sellout streak began with a 16–7 loss to Missouri on November 3, 1962, when 36,501 showed up to see the game. Incredibly, that streak is still going.

Through the 2007 season, Nebraska has sold out 289 consecutive home games, a continuing NCAA record. In 2006 a 6,500-seat addition in the north of Memorial Stadium, along with a massive HuskerVision Screen and Skyline Suites ushered in the first crowds of more than 80,000 people at home games.

chapter 2
Early Success

Nebraska defensive end Ivan Zimmer (86), swoops in on Missouri quarterback Gary Lane (16) on October 30, 1965, in Columbia, Missouri.

Buoyed by their first bowl victory in history in 1962, Bob Devaney's Huskers in 1963 would become Nebraska's first conference football champion since 1940. Led by all-conference players—quarterback Dennis Claridge, guard Bob Brown, and tackle Lloyd Voss—the Cornhuskers finally beat Oklahoma and won the league championship in OU coach Bud Wilkinson's final season.

Once OU's league domination had ended, and Nebraska figured out how to beat Missouri, the Cornhuskers went to two Orange Bowls, a Cotton Bowl, and a Sugar Bowl, and laid a foundation for the rest of the millennium.

Over that four-year period, from 1963 to 1966, Nebraska won four straight outright Big Eight titles, posted a 26–2 league record, and had a 38–6 overall mark. Eight Nebraska players were selected as All-Americans during that four-year period: tackles Larry Kramer and Walt Barnes; ends Tony Jeter and Freeman White; guards Brown, Wayne Meylan, and LaVerne Allers; and defensive back Larry Wachholtz.

Nebraska's Smallish Fullback Frank Solich

Solich, the spunky, squat-sized, 158-pound running back from Cleveland, Ohio, led Nebraska in rushing and all-purpose yards as a junior in 1964. And he led Nebraska in kickoff returns three straight seasons, from 1963 to 1965, punt returns in 1964, and all-purpose yards in 1965.

"I got recruited on the defensive side of the ball first, and then as a halfback for a little bit, and then at fullback," Solich said. "I thought Coach Devaney maybe had lost his marbles a little bit when he put me at fullback. But they had a system in place that was an unbalanced line and a full-house backfield. And the halfbacks were right around 200 or over. We would run an isolation play, where the lead halfback would go through and block the linebacker, and the fullback would carry the ball. It was really kind of a reverse of the I formation in that regard.

"If you ran a power play, the lead halfback would block a defensive end, and I would run through and block the itty-bitty corner," Solich added. "It was somewhat in reverse of the I in how it worked. I ended up with a broken ankle my sophomore year. I had a shoulder operation after my junior year and a knee operation after my senior year. So it took its toll."

On leading Nebraska in kickoff returns three straight seasons, Solich said, "I think they tried to plug me in and use me where they could. I did return punts for a while. I think I was a sophomore when I dropped a punt against Oklahoma and I had to scramble to recover it. I didn't see much of returning punts after that."

Rolling in 1963

Except for a stumble against Air Force (17–13) in Lincoln in early October when a long pass beat the Cornhuskers, Nebraska was perfect during the 1963 season. Devaney ended Nebraska's six-year losing streak against Missouri with a 13–12 victory in Columbia and then beat Wilkinson and the Sooners in the crucial season finale, 29–20, also in Lincoln.

The Nebraska-Oklahoma game was one of the few scheduled games to go ahead as planned, a day after the assassination of President John F. Kennedy in Dallas on November 22, 1963. The Big Eight's Missouri-Kansas game, as an example, like most other college games, was postponed a week.

"I was 34," said then Big Eight Commissioner Wayne Duke. "But I was 64 by the end of the week. The Orange Bowl had terminated our contract. On Friday, Kennedy was shot. This was Bud's last game. He had resigned. He was seeking a seat in the U.S. Senate and would get beat by Fred Harris.

"Bud had gotten a hold of Bobby Kennedy. Bud was close to Kennedy. Bobby told Bud to go ahead and play the game. Very few games were played that day. He was saying to Bud that the country was in turmoil [and the game should be played]. There was talk about [how maybe] Cuban interests had shot Kennedy.

There were so many uncertainties. There were only one or two games played in the country. I wanted to make sure that Bud was telling me the truth. I talked to Bobby Kennedy, and he said, 'Yes, I did say that.' Bud had been on John Kennedy's Physical Fitness Committee."

The Board of Regents at Nebraska, in consultation with Duke, Nebraska state officials, and the coaches, made the announcement on Friday night the show would go on as planned.

Both Nebraska and Oklahoma were unbeaten in league play, and this game would decide the Big Eight championship. The eventual result was rather startling.

The Cornhuskers led only 3–0 at halftime, then manhandled the Sooners in the second half with four touchdowns. Nebraska jumped to a 29–7 lead before Devaney sent in the reserves against the fumbling Sooners.

But aside from Nebraska earning a berth in the Orange Bowl against Auburn was the fact that Big Eight schools in the future would have a freer rein to go to other bowls. This promoted growth in the league and helped Nebraska, which would play in the Cotton and Sugar Bowls in two of the following three seasons.

The Big Eight agreement with the Orange Bowl had dictated the league send a team to Miami. Oklahoma, as league champion, had gone to four Orange Bowls from 1954 to 1959—and probably would have gone to a fifth on January 1, 1955, had the bowl not had a no-repeat rule from the previous season when the Sooners had shut out Maryland 7–0.

Nebraska actually went to the Orange Bowl after the 1954 season as the second-place Big 7 team behind champion Oklahoma. But the Cornhuskers had lost to the Sooners 55–7, and entered the 1955 Orange Bowl with a 6–4 overall record. They lost to Duke 34–7 in Miami. After that game, the Orange Bowl repealed its no-repeat rule.

But by the early 1960s, Big Eight teams, other than the champion, were starting to go to some other bowls. As a result, after the 1963 season, the Big Eight wouldn't be guaranteed a slot in Miami as it had been since the 1953 season (1954 Orange Bowl).

"Ted O'Leary was a stringer for *Sports Illustrated* then in Kansas City, and he wrote it was going to be the death penalty to Big Eight football," Duke said of the termination of the Orange Bowl agreement. "Quite to the contrary, it proved to be a boon for Big Eight football. At the time, the Big Eight was known as 'OU and the Seven Dwarfs.' Bud [Wilkinson] was dominating the conference. He would go out and recruit, and we didn't have teams going to other bowl games. No longer could Oklahoma recruit and say, 'Come with us. The only bowl we go to is the Orange Bowl, and we go every time.' After that, six out of eight years I was Big Eight commissioner, we still [had a team] that played in the Orange Bowl. But we went to other bowl games. It proved to be an equalizer in the Big Eight."

The other major development that helped Nebraska during this era was the evolving season-ending television schedule. Duke played a part in this as well.

Duke said he, NCAA executive director Walter Byers, and ABC-TV executive Roone Arledge had a discussion after an NCAA Television Committee meeting to discuss what they could do to promote college football on Thanksgiving Day, which was dominated by professional football. The idea was to move the Nebraska-Oklahoma game, usually scheduled at the end of the season anyway, to Thanksgiving afternoon. And people could watch the game either before, during, or after they ate their turkey.

"Gomer Jones [the Oklahoma coach in 1964 and 1965, following Wilkinson] and Bob Devaney could have cared less," Duke said of the 1965 season schedule change.

So for the first time, Nebraska-Oklahoma was played and shown nationally on network television on November 25, 1965. Nebraska won 21–9 over a mediocre OU team and claimed the Big Eight title by a game over Missouri. The game would be on national television the next two seasons on Thanksgiving, with Oklahoma winning both times. The game was later moved to Friday after Thanksgiving and sometimes played on Saturday. But the television element had been introduced and set apart these two Big Eight powers for the next three decades as often meeting in a glamorous season-ending game on network television. It proved to be a huge recruiting advantage for both programs.

The 1963 Season Ends with the Orange Bowl

The 1964 Orange Bowl game at the end of the 1963 season was the last played during the day before NBC snapped up the television contract from ABC and moved it to prime time. Nebraska knocked off Auburn 13–7 on January 1, 1964, and claimed the first of four victories by Bob Devaney in his five Orange Bowl appearances. This was Nebraska's first New Year's Day bowl victory. And it was predictably close because Nebraska and Auburn were both ranked either fifth or sixth in the two major polls.

Nebraska quarterback Dennis Claridge, who later became a dentist, came up huge early in this game. A 6'4", 220-pounder, Claridge was a powerful yet nifty runner. And on the second play from scrimmage, he went right, followed his blockers, then got to the sideline. He covered 68 yards for a touchdown on a play designed for short yardage to stake the Cornhuskers to a 7–0 lead. At the time, it was the longest touchdown run in Orange Bowl history.

Nebraska, which led the country in rushing yards (262.6 per game) in 1963, added two short field goals in the first half by Dave Theisen, both the longest at the time in Orange Bowl history as well, the first from 31 yards then 36 yards. Trailing 13–0, Auburn finally scored in the third quarter when 6'3", 210-pound quarterback Jimmy Sidle ran in from 13 yards out. Sidle was one of the top running quarterbacks in the country, but also was a good passer and tagged the Cornhuskers for 157 yards through the air.

Nebraska didn't secure the victory until linebacker John Kirby swatted away Sidle's fourth-down pass at the goal line with less than three minutes remaining in the game.

Off Devaney's 1963 Nebraska team, nine players were drafted, including Brown, who was picked in the first round by Philadelphia, and Voss, who was a first-round selection by Green

Dennis Claridge (14) romps for a 68-yard touchdown run on the second play of the Orange Bowl on January 1, 1964, against Auburn.

Bay. That was the highest number of Nebraska players selected in the NFL Draft until 10 were picked off the 1972 Big Eight title team that beat Notre Dame in the Orange Bowl.

Devaney's Recruiting, Practice Wizardry

Barry Alvarez arrived as a freshman linebacker in the fall of 1964 and was a prime example of Devaney's recruiting abilities. Coming from the Midwest, Devaney was going back into Ohio and then to Pennsylvania and finally to New Jersey and California. Later, Tom Osborne would stretch the Nebraska recruiting into Texas and Florida.

Of course, Nebraska would also develop a tremendous walk-on program. But because Nebraska was not a populous state, it was often necessary to travel far and wide for recruits.

"John Melton [a Nebraska assistant coach] was from my hometown," said Alvarez, who hailed from Burgettstown,

Pennsylvania. "What they did pretty much, they worked the Midwest and they worked areas where coaches had relationships and recruited those areas. He signed a great player in Tony Jeter [an end from West Virginia], Harry Wilson [halfback from Ohio], Ted Vactor [halfback from Pennsylvania]. All those guys were a little before me. The year before they recruited me, they played in the Orange Bowl. My eyes lit up when they played in the Orange Bowl. I wanted to play in bowl games."

Devaney was at the center of recruiting. End Tony Jeter wound up being a dual All-American (football and academics). He recalled in a 1996 interview with the *Dallas Morning News* that Devaney was in his home when his mother sat down at the organ. The Irish coach promptly accompanied the mother in song. Mother decided right then where Jeter was going to school.

"I was going to play for that nice Mr. Devaney," said Jeter.

Once at Nebraska, Alvarez said he was playing for a coach who was years ahead of the curve.

"Well, first of all, I really felt at a very young age I was playing for someone very special, the way he practiced," said Alvarez, current Wisconsin athletics director and former Badgers head coach. "It was revolutionary in those days. He was way ahead of his time. Down South they were killing guys when they would lose a game. They would punish them. His practices were much more structured. There were no scrimmages during the season. His practices then are how they are today. There was a lot of teaching. There was individual work, group work, then to the whole. It was part groups to whole. There was more teaching than banging."

Alvarez said Devaney was a person after whom he patterned his entire career after his playing days because Devaney was so good at what he did.

"I really looked up to him," Alvarez continued. "Like how he set up his program out of season, his philosophy, and why he did things. He gave me a foundation I worked off of. I worked with some very good coaches, but Devaney gave me a foundation and a direction to follow. I tried to follow the path he took, coaching in high school. I started as a high school coach and assistant coach on the college level. And if I was lucky enough to get hired at a Division I school, then eventually I wanted to become an administrator. I followed that path. And I remember his dual roles [as an athletics director/coach at Nebraska]. When he stepped down as head coach, he had taken no pay for the athletics director's role when he was coach, so when he took the athletics director's job, his salary stayed the same."

Winding Up in Dallas

In 1964 Nebraska won its second straight Big Eight title as preseason favorite Oklahoma floundered in the early part of the season under new head coach Gomer Jones. Under Jones, a former Wilkinson assistant promoted to the head job, the Sooners lost to Southern California and Texas in nonconference games and to Kansas by a point. An Oklahoma tie with Missouri meant the Sooners couldn't beat out an unbeaten Nebraska team for the Big Eight title when the two teams met in Norman in late November.

Nebraska, led by All-American tackle Larry Kramer, had mowed down nine straight opponents with a tough defense and a ground-oriented offense spearheaded by Solich and quarterback Bob Churchich. The Cornhuskers led OU 7–3 going into the fourth quarter, but Oklahoma put together an 88-yard scoring drive and then scored on a long run to win 17–7.Because the Big Eight no longer was guaranteed a slot in the Orange Bowl, Nebraska went to the Cotton Bowl, and second-place Oklahoma to the Gator Bowl.

For a second straight season, Nebraska finished among the top 10 teams in the country.

But the Cotton Bowl would begin a three-game postseason tailspin for Devaney, who wouldn't win another bowl game until after the 1969 season. A 10–7 loss to Arkansas was similar to the season-ending loss to Oklahoma. Nebraska's defense wouldn't budge most of the game—until the end.

Halfback Harry Wilson scored Nebraska's lone touchdown on a one-yard run early in the second quarter after Arkansas had taken a 3–0 lead in the first quarter. Wilson said after the game, "I just ran over the defensive man on that touchdown. We ran the same play twice in succession." That was Nebraska power football at its best. *Just try and stop us.*

His Razorbacks trailing 7–3 at halftime, Arkansas coach Frank Broyles said, "Didn't have to tell them anything. They were telling each other. Nebraska was big and strong. So we had to gamble a lot, and when we guessed wrong, we looked bad. I know how they feel. It happened to us four years ago [in a 7–6 loss to Duke] here. We were ahead until the last. It was our fourth try [at winning a Cotton Bowl game]."

Arkansas scored on a three-yard touchdown by Bobby Burnett with 4:41 remaining on an 80-yard, nine-play drive. The big play on the drive was a 28-yard pass caught by 6′2″ wingback Jim Lindsey, taking the ball to the Cornhuskers' 5-yard line.

"Yes, we set up that pass to the tailback because we just couldn't handle their ends on the big rush," Broyles said. "We had thrown to the tailback before, but always when he was in motion first."

Nebraska finished the season ranked sixth in the country. Arkansas wound up number two in the AP and UPI Polls behind Alabama, but won its only national championship in football when it was crowned number one by the Football Writers Association of America when Alabama was upset by Texas in the Orange Bowl.

Devaney's Third Straight Title

Nebraska had it really going by this time

"In those early years there was an unlimited amount of scholarships," linebacker Barry Alvarez remembers. "They were bringing guys in by the truckloads. Spring practice was like a death march. At times there were so many guys in shifts, the first three teams would scrimmage in the morning, and the fourth and fifth would scrimmage in the afternoon. If you were not close to the two-deep after the spring, you would have to decide where to go the next year, like South Dakota or Drake. Nebraska would help place them. The spring scrimmage was serious."

Nebraska's hard-nosed, stingy defenders became known as the "Blackshirts." Alvarez remembers how that name was acquired purely by accident.

"George Kelly and Mike Corgan went down to a sporting goods store to by some pullovers," Alvarez said. "They went down there and the only colors they had were black, yellow, and green. George took black ones, and the first-team defense wore them and made a big deal about it."

Nebraska's offense was precision-like and hard-nosed as well. And the linemen were standouts.

"Wayne Meylan was unbelievable," Alvarez said. "He was unbelievably strong and never lifted weights. He could run as fast as the backs. Freeman White was a freaky athlete. We had a lot of good football players."

In the 1965 season Solich had the best rushing game of any fullback in Nebraska history, a mark that still stands today. Solich gained 204 yards and scored three touchdowns against the Falcons in a 27–17 victory in Colorado Springs.

"There was some question about an inadvertent whistle," Solich said. "I had a run where Air Force complained that some of their players heard a whistle and some of them stopped. None of the officials recognized any of it.

"After the game in the locker room, Devaney said, 'It is a good thing we are a little deaf of hearing, isn't it Frank?' He might have heard the whistle. I am not sure," Solich said, laughing. "But it really wasn't that difficult. I had three or four long plays they broke real clean. At the end of the game, it didn't seem like I had done much."

Solich scored on touchdown runs of 20, 80, and 59 yards—the latter when the inadvertent whistle might have blown. Solich's 204 yards rushing broke the previous single-game rushing mark of 187 yards by Bobby Reynolds in 1950. No other Husker had a better rushing game until Rick Berns (211 yards) in 1976.

"Solich was playing with two halfbacks in a full-house back-field," Alvarez said. "And those two halfbacks weighed 240 pounds. They were the lead backs. Frank was not leading on any blocks."

Nebraska finished the 1965 regular season with a 10–0 record. Oklahoma was in a weakened state in the second and last season under Gomer Jones and slipped to fifth place in the Big Eight. Missouri was the second-place pursuer and lost a 16–14 thriller to the Cornhuskers in Columbia. But equally big was a 21–17 Nebraska victory over Oklahoma State and running back Walt Garrison in Stillwater in the ninth game of the season.

Garrison, who later would play for the Dallas Cowboys, was nearly unstoppable, carrying the ball 19 times for 121 yards. On the last play of the game, he ran 18 yards and was stopped at the Nebraska 5-yard line by several Blackshirt defenders. Nebraska left Stillwater with a hard-earned victory.

"I remember it was a long run and that Walt Garrison was running all over the field," said Alvarez. "It was the first time [guard] Wayne Meylan had played. He had only played defense a week. He had started the season on offense. He had moved ahead of Jerry Murphy. I can remember him jumping on Walt Garrison's back. All day we couldn't block [Garrison]."

Nebraska's perfect season was saved when the Cornhuskers scored on a three-yard run by fullback Pete Tatman late in the game, after Oklahoma State had taken a 17–14 lead with 5:19 to play.

After the game, third-ranked Nebraska accepted a bid to play in the Orange Bowl, with the probable opponent expected to be fourth-ranked Alabama. It would be the first of three postseason meetings between Devaney and Bear Bryant in bowl games.

Alabama's Orange Bowl Chicanery

When top-ranked Michigan State lost to UCLA in the Rose Bowl and number-two Arkansas fell to LSU in the Cotton Bowl, the national title was at stake when number-three Nebraska and number-four Alabama played in Nebraska's first night bowl game in Miami, Florida, at the Orange Bowl.

"The thing I remember about the Orange Bowl versus Alabama, it seems like they set a record for onside kicking, recovering onside kicks, which was really vital to the course of winning the football game," Solich said.

Bryant knew he had to change his strategy and try and outscore Nebraska, because the Cornhuskers were one of the top scoring teams in the country. Bryant told only his starting quarterback about his change in strategy and swore him to secrecy.

Years later, Steve Sloan, then the Crimson Tide quarterback that year, recalled the conversation he had with Bryant on an Orange Bowl–sponsored cruise for players and coaches prior to the game with the Cornhuskers.

"Coach Bryant was pretty conservative," Sloan said, "He played for field position, emphasized the kicking game. But he told me, 'Look, you just throw the ball any time you feel like it.' I said, 'Coach, are you serious?' And he said he was because, 'This is the only team we've played in years that I don't think we can stop.'"

Sloan, given the green light to throw no matter where he was on the field, attempted more passes in the first half than he usually did in the game. And the strategy caught Nebraska completely off guard. The powerful Cornhuskers fell behind 24–7 in the first half and could never recover in a 39–28 loss to the Crimson Tide.

"Bryant outcoached us," Alvarez said. "We were the better team."

Sloan took Alabama on a scoring drive on its initial possession of the game, hitting end Ray Perkins on a 32-yard touchdown pass. He followed up with another scoring toss to Perkins in the first half. By the end of the game, Sloan had completed 20 passes for 296 yards, both Orange Bowl records at the time. Perkins caught nine passes for 159 yards, also Orange Bowl records at the time.

Despite Nebraska quarterback Bob Churchich playing a part in all of Nebraska's points—passing for three touchdowns and a PAT and running for another touchdown—the 39 points would be the second most given up by a Bob Devaney team at Nebraska during his 11-year tenure at Lincoln, a span of 123 games.

Alabama, as a result of the upset, moved past Michigan State, Arkansas, and Nebraska, and was crowned number one in the Associated Press poll, which for the first time was taken after the bowls. UPI had named Michigan State number one in its final poll before the bowls.

The 1966 Season

Nebraska ran its regular-season winning streak to 19 games by winning the first nine games of the 1966 season before meeting Oklahoma in the season finale that year. The early games were often close, though, causing UCLA coach Tommy Prothro to tell a Los Angeles newspaper man that, "Nebraska should be ranked 49th instead of eighth." Devaney got hold of the article and put it on the bulletin board before the Missouri game in Lincoln. And it obviously served as motivation. Nebraska crushed the Tigers 35–0.

But Nebraska's lack of speed at running back would eventually catch up with the Cornhuskers. Wilson and fellow running back Ben Gregory were strong runners. But Nebraska lacked a speed back.

"Harry Wilson was a great back," Alvarez said. "He could block and he could also make you miss. He got a little heavy his senior year. But he was a great back. He was the package. He would have played a long time in the NFL had he not gotten injured."

Oklahoma upset Nebraska 10–9 in the 10th game. But because Jim Mackenzie's only OU team (he died of a heart attack after the 1966 season) was in the middle of the standings, Nebraska still won the Big 8 title with a game to spare over Colorado.

The Nebraska-Colorado game turned out to be the pivotal Big Eight game that season. Nebraska prevailed 21–19 over the Buffaloes in Colorado, rallying from a 19–7 deficit in the fourth quarter. Churchich scored to make it 19–14 Colorado after a 72-yard drive with 10 minutes left. Late in the game, NU drove to the 9-yard line. And three plays later, Nebraska scored on a two-yard run by Pete Tatman with 53 seconds remaining for the victory.

Nebraska, ranked sixth, wound up playing number-three Alabama in a bowl for the second straight season, but this time in the Sugar Bowl. The impending result would change everything for Bob Devaney.

chapter 3
Down Years

*Alabama quarterback Kenny Stabler blows
out the candles on the birthday cake upon
arrival in New Orleans on December 25,
1966, before blowing out Nebraska in the
1967 Sugar Bowl. Looking on at left is
Alabama coach Paul "Bear" Bryant.*

Nebraska lost the 1967 Sugar Bowl to Alabama 34–7, the second-worst loss during the Bob Devaney era in Lincoln and the third-highest point total given up. Nebraska appeared to be a big, lumbering, slow team that was swarmed by a quicker Alabama team bent on winning a share of the national title.

Devaney had wanted a rematch with Bear Bryant from the previous season's loss in the Orange Bowl when the Cornhuskers believed they had just been outfoxed by quarterback Steve Sloan's surprise passing barrage and Alabama's onside kicks.

The Sugar Bowl rematch was a severe disappointment to Devaney, who watched as the more nimble Crimson Tide mounted a 24–0 lead in the first half. This time the Alabama quarterback was Kenny Stabler, who would go on to become a big star with the Oakland Raiders.

A crowd of 82,000 at old Tulane Stadium watched as Alabama jumped to a 17–0 lead, which included a 14-yard run by Stabler, who finished with 218 yards passing. Alabama led 27–0 before Nebraska could score early in the fourth quarter on quarterback Bob Churchich's 15-yard pass to Dick Davis.

Stabler merely answered with the final points in the game on a 45-yard pass to Ray Perkins, who had caught two touchdown passes in the previous year's bowl-game victory over Nebraska.

The Big Eight's wide-open bowl policy had been a double-edged sword for the Cornhuskers, who had won four straight titles from 1963 through 1966. They got to play in the Cotton and Sugar Bowls after the 1964 and 1966 seasons, respectively. But they lost both of those games, sandwiched around the Orange Bowl loss to Alabama after the 1965 season.

As a result, Nebraska joined Alabama as the only other team to have the distinction of losing in all four of the major New Year's Day bowl games as of that season. Nebraska had managed to slip into the spotlight, but then slip on a banana peel each time. The Cornhuskers were 1–5 in those New Year's Day games, including defeats to Stanford (21–13) in the 1941 Rose Bowl and to Duke (34–7) in the 1955 Orange Bowl.

Devaney had lost three straight New Year's Day games since the 13–7 victory over Auburn in the 1964 Orange Bowl. Clearly, he believed he needed to rethink his program's philosophy if Nebraska was to ever win a national title. How could Nebraska match Alabama's speed?

"They [the Crimson Tide] were just better, so he [Devaney] wanted guys to lose weight and work on quickness," said linebacker Barry Alvarez, who would be one of the defensive stars of the 1967 season along with middle guard Wayne Meylan, tackle Jim McCord, and cornerbacks Jim Hawkins and Dana Stephenson.

The Weight-Loss Experiment Backfires

"Alabama looked at us as a bunch of big, slow guys from the North, and they were fast, quick guys from the South," said former NU linebacker Adrian Fiala. "They aimed to beat us and they did. But as a result of that, Bob Devaney changed his philosophy. When we got done with that game, the Sugar Bowl, the 1966 season, the next few weeks before conditioning got under way, we were all told what you had to lose in terms of weight. And everybody was put on a program to lose weight. And when you are playing in the Big Eight and you are undersized, things happen, and they are not good."

Fiala said as a result of the weight loss, which might have ranged from 10 to 15 pounds a player, Nebraska couldn't enforce its will anymore on offense. Its offensive line lacked power, and its skilled players' lacked strength because of the weight loss—although the defense played fine and remained aggressive.

In 1967, for the first time since Devaney's first season of 1962, Nebraska would not lead the Big Eight in total offense. The Cornhuskers had led the conference with 347.6 offensive yards a game in 1963, 348.5 in 1964, 404.0 in 1965, and 318.8 in 1966. The figure dropped to 317.1 yards a game in

1967, when Nebraska became more of a passing team with quarterback Frank Patrick.

But it was almost by necessity. In 1967 Nebraska rushed for just 162.5 yards a game, 30 yards less than the previous season and 1275 yards less than in 1965, when it led the country with 290 rushing yards a game.

"When you lose 10 to 15 pounds, yeah, you feel lighter, and you feel like you can go faster," Fiala said. "Are you? I don't know. And a lot of that had to do with the fact our offense wasn't very good at all in 1967 and 1968. And our offensive line, that is where the weight thing really came to bear....We got shoved around quite a bit."

Nebraska's point production really fell off—in 1967 to 12.7 points a game, down from 21.6 in 1966 and 32.1 in 1965, when it ranked second in the country in scoring behind Arkansas (32.4). And in 1968 Nebraska's scoring barely improved to 15.5 points a game. As a result, Nebraska scored more than 17 points just once in 1967, tumbled to 3–4 in the Big Eight (a fifth-place tie) and 6–4 overall. The 1968 season was nearly a mirror image: 6–4 overall and 3–4 in the conference (a fourth-place tie).

Devaney was concerned about job security at that point, especially after Oklahoma posted a 47–0 victory over Nebraska in the 1968 season finale. It was the worst loss during the Devaney era at Nebraska and obviously a low point of his regime.

"They were phenomenal winners when he first came," former NU assistant coach Jim Walden said of the 1962 through 1966 teams. "They had two 6–4 seasons. In 1969 they were a little nervous. They had a feeling they could lose their jobs."

Still the Rib-Rattling Defense

Despite the problems on offense, Nebraska's Blackshirts had prospered in 1967 when Alvarez was a senior and Fiala was a sophomore. The Cornhuskers led the country in total defense (157.6 yards allowed a game) and also in pass defense (90.1

yards allowed a game). And Nebraska was not too shabby on rush defense in 1967, either, permitting just 67.5 rushing yards a game. It was the fifth-straight season Devaney's Cornhuskers had led the Big Eight in rushing defense.

Meylan was an overpowering force in the middle. In 1967 alone Meylan had 119 total tackles (59 unassisted). And if Meylan didn't tackle somebody, Alvarez probably did (112 tackles, 34 unassisted). Meylan was selected in the fourth round by the Cleveland Browns in the 1968 draft and played three seasons in the NFL, while Alvarez headed into coaching ranks and eventually became head coach at Wisconsin.

"Barry is one of the best people you ever want to know. He is a very considerate guy," Fiala said. "He always has the best interests of people at heart. He always tried to get the job done the right way. Playing with him was the same way. I was a couple of years behind him. But he kind of took me under his wing. And he helped me early in my career and gave me encouragement. So it came as no surprise to me he was so good at recruiting [when he was the Wisconsin coach] because he could relate to players very well."

The 1968 season would be the last time Nebraska lost four times in a season for a period of 30 years—until 1998 when Frank Solich's first team finished 9–4. In 1968 Nebraska lost to both Kansas and Kansas State in the same season. And that wouldn't happen at any time for the rest of the millennium. Nebraska beat Kansas State 29 consecutive seasons (until 1998) and Kansas for 36 straight seasons (until 2005).

"I think in 1968, out of 22 Kansas State starters, 10 or 11 of us were sophomores," remembers Kansas State quarterback Lynn Dickey, who later went on to star in the NFL. "We were all too stupid to be scared. I remember walking into [Nebraska's] stadium and thinking I had never seen so much red in my life. Our defense played really well. It snowed that game. I hit Dave Jones with a long pass on the first play of the game. And a couple of plays later I passed to Mack Herron for a touchdown. We kicked two field goals and won 12–0."

Junior College Linemen, Weight Lifting

After the 1968 season, Devaney changed directions again. He went into the western junior college ranks to recruit linemen. And he eventually became a believer in weight lifting as a means to develop players with strength and quickness when Boyd Epley entered the Nebraska football program.

"Our weight-training room was a stock room off the training room," said Jim Walden, who was an NU assistant coach during that era. "Coach Devaney was not of the era of weight training. His off-season running and conditioning—jumping dummies and playing racquetball—was the forerunner of winter programs. We would have eight stations. We had ropes and dummies, another group doing drills, another group running. We would do 40-minute workouts, three days a week. There would be eight stations, five minutes each."

But in the late 1960s and early 1970s, Devaney brought in offensive line standouts from the California and other western junior colleges—Bob Newton (La Mirada, California), Carl Johnson (Phoenix, Arizona), Dick Rupert (Los Angeles, California), and Keith Wortman (Whittier, California). They all ended up being All–Big Eight and/or were drafted into pro football.

"They were really good players," Alvarez said. "They helped us get over the hump."

"What they brought was weight training, which was big then on the West Coast. They were lifters," Walden said. "Boyd Epley was a pole vaulter on our Nebraska track team. He had hurt his back. And he was doing well lifting. He got in with those California kids. And Coach Devaney put two and two together. He saw how strong they were and how much they liked to lift. There was a correlation. Boyd asked for more space and weights, and he got it. There were some good athletes there after two 6–4 seasons. There was a combination of junior-college kids, weight training, and some really good football players. The 1969 team benefited from that."

Epley is modest when discussing the situation.

"They were looking for something to turn them around," Epley said in a 1996 interview. "They made a lot of changes at that time. I am not saying it was the reason they started winning, but it had something to do with it.

"And nobody got slower. They all got faster."

Tom Osborne, then an assistant coach, initially summoned Epley.

"But he [Devaney] was the boss," Epley added. "He had the offensive line coach there with him. But Bob Devaney, being the head coach, he still had to make the decision whether it was mandatory or optional. He said this first year we will make it optional, but if anybody gets slower, you are out of a job."

When Epley started the weight program, the bench press was the most popular exercise, but that would change as well.

"I didn't have the benefit of scientific research back then," Epley said. "The only resources available to me were the existing weight-lifting groups—the power lifters, the Olympic lifters, and the body builders. So from 1970 to 1972, I competed in each of those areas myself and tried to gain as much information as to what was different for each one and what would be useful to athletes. Athletes didn't lift weights back then. Weight lifters were some kind of subculture. I tried to pull out of those areas what I thought were good and used those to help people.

"Over time, we realized the bench press was way overrated for the sport of football," Epley continued. "We didn't even have it as part of our testing. [The squat and hang cleans are more important] because your feet are on the ground and you use multiple joints. When you compete in athletics, your feet are on the ground and you use multiple joints." These lifting exercises emphasize getting the power athletes need in their lower bodies for football.

Over the years, Epley incorporated nutrition into the mix. And Nebraska increased and improved its weight-training and fitness facilities. Those now rank among the best, largest, and most sophisticated in the country.

Also in the late 1960s, Nebraska also added great skilled players to go along with the improvements in weight training.

"We had great speed," Alvarez said. "We had two recruiting years where we added Johnny Rodgers [wingback], Jerry Tagge [quarterback], Van Brownson [quarterback], Jeff Kinney [half-back], Larry Jacobson [defensive tackle], and Rich Glover [middle guard]....All those guys came in those two years. We had tremendous skilled players and outstanding quarterbacks. I thought Jeff Kinney was the best player on the team. He started at tailback, but he could have played quarterback or safety. He kicked and did everything."

"In 1969 we got an offensive back [Kinney], we got our size back, and we were cochampions with Missouri in 1969," Fiala said. "Jerry Tagge arrived. Van Brownson and Jeff Kinney arrived. And Larry Jacobson. And people like that. They were sophomores. So we added some very good talent to what we had."

During that 1969 season, probably the best player of all was just a freshman. He would not become eligible until the 1970 season as a sophomore

"Johnny Rodgers was on the freshmen football team," said Fiala, who was a senior in 1969. "On Mondays the lower varsity units would scrimmage the freshmen. So we would have a short practice on Monday and get cleaned up and kind of watch the fourth and fifth teams go against the freshmen. Johnny, offensively we knew what he could do. But Johnny was a really good defensive back. As a matter of fact, I have always told people [he was] a complete player, who could play either side of the ball, could throw the ball, he could even kick pretty well. Johnny was probably the most complete football player of anybody I have seen. He never played defensive back in a varsity game or kicked."

Walden saw Rodgers every day in practice.

"Jim Ross and I were the freshman coaches," he said. "We played four freshman games in 1969. It was hard to describe J.R. He was like nothing I had seen before. He turned tackle into touch football. He was 5'8", 5'9" and 145, 150 pounds. He would catch a punt...it was just unbelievable. He was a little man among boys at some point. The varsity guys were getting a chip on their shoulders, but they saw he was really the real deal when he moved up that spring of 1970."

chapter 4
Back-to-Back National Titles, Game of the Century

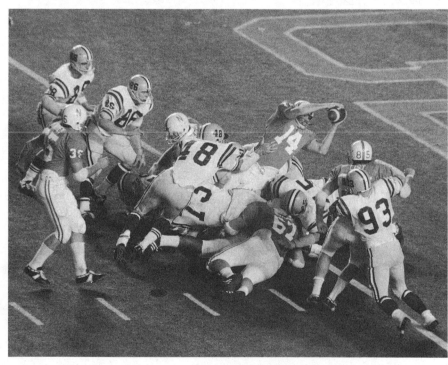

Jerry Tagge, shown here plunging over the pileup at the goal line in the 1971 Orange Bowl against LSU, and his classmates who arrived in the late 1960s marked a new era for the Huskers.

Nebraska kicked off the 1970 season with a 36–12 victory over Wake Forest in which sophomore Johnny Rodgers made his varsity debut. He would be the final link to Nebraska's first consensus national championship in 1971.

With Jerry Tagge and Van Brownson at quarterback, Jeff Kinney at running back, Rodgers at wingback, and a big offensive line, Nebraska had a spectacular offense in 1970. Future Outland Trophy–winning tackle Larry Jacobson, star linebacker Jerry Murtaugh, and future All-American end Willie Harper were the defensive stars.

Nebraska had a big advantage on offense because the Cornhuskers could play two quarterbacks with different styles.

"You loved them both," said Jim Walden, who was a Nebraska assistant coach in that era. "They could do 70 percent of the same things. But Van Brownson could do some things Tagge couldn't. Van Brownson was superior at options. Tagge was a little bit better thrower in certain situations. In some ways, they were very different. Van Brownson was more of a Jim Walden–style gambler, more an out-of-the-box type guy. He was an attention-getter. Tagge was a model of consistency. He was a big, heavy-legged Wisconsin kid. Van Brownson was excellent running the pass-bootleg. Tagge was stronger and better in the cup [pocket]."

Rodgers, a wingback, was probably the most dynamic player to hit college football for a variety of reasons: his quickness, speed, durability, and versatility. He had great ability to slip out of tackles and run as fast laterally as he could straight ahead. He could single-handedly turn a game around on special teams. And he could show up on the field in various positions, creating nightmares for defensive coordinators. Over the course of his career, Rodgers would set a then–NCAA record for all-purpose yards with 5,586.

"He might just be the greatest college player of all-time," said former Kansas State coach Vince Gibson.

With the addition of Omaha's Rodgers, who would encounter trouble with the law for a service station holdup after his sophomore season but never be dismissed from the team by a forgiving Devaney,

Nebraska would post a 33–2–2 record from 1970 to 1972, including two unbeaten seasons that resulted in national titles.

The first of these was 1970 when Nebraska finished 11–0–1. The only blemish was a 21–21 tie against third-ranked USC in Los Angeles when the Trojans rallied to tie Nebraska. Nebraska blew away other teams, except 21–7 over Missouri; 29–13 at Colorado, and 28–21 over Oklahoma.

The Missouri game was huge because Dan Devine's Tigers had beaten Nebraska in tight, defensive struggles the previous three seasons–10–7,16–14, and 17–7.And this one was another one of those with the score tied 7–7 in the second half. But when Missouri's sensational tailback Joe Moore suffered a college career–ending injury, the fire seemed to leave the Tigers, and Nebraska prevailed in Lincoln for a 4–0–1 start.

Colorado in Boulder was giving Nebraska a game. A huge play occurred when Jacobson saved a touchdown when he tackled speedy Cliff Branch on a reverse on the 1-yard line.

Nebraska, at 10–0–1, was ranked third in the country going into an Orange Bowl date with number-five LSU. On the surface, it appeared that this bowl would not be for the national title and that the USC tie had cost Nebraska dearly. United Press International already had named Texas number one in its final poll before the bowls. But the Associated Press poll still was out there.

Then the dominoes started to fall on New Year's Day. Notre Dame upset top-ranked Texas in the Cotton Bowl. And number-two Ohio State lost a shocker to Stanford in the Rose Bowl. By the time the Cornhuskers took the field that night, they knew they could win the national title in one poll with a victory.

"Our team was ready, too,"said LSU coach Charlie McClendon in *Fifty Years on the Fifty: The Orange Bowl Story.* "But when they came out of the dressing room, they were so high, I don't think they touched the ground until they got to the 50-yard line."

Nebraska took a 10–0 first-quarter lead and led 10–3 at the half. But LSU stormed back with another field goal and finally a touchdown on the last play of the third quarter to take a 12–10 lead (the kick failed).

Tagge then took Nebraska on its national championship–winning drive of 67 yards. But the last inches were all Tagge, with 8:50 left in the game on a make-or-break fourth-down play at the LSU 1.

"LSU was a tough, tough battle," Walden said. "They were a big, typical SEC team. They could throw the ball....I will always remember the quarterback sneak by Tagge and him holding the ball over. I remember how darn tough it was to play LSU. And I had such great respect for their coach, Charlie McClendon. He and Bob were so much alike—fun guys. Tagge checked to the sneak. LSU got caught out of position. That was the difference in the ballgame. I remember how hard it was played. The guys were just playing their butts off."

It took a couple of big defensive plays by the Blackshirts to seal the deal. Harper stole the ball from the LSU quarterback to stop one drive. And NU linebacker Bob Terrio intercepted a pass to stop another to batten down a 17–12 Nebraska win.

Jeff Kinney goes over the top for a one-yard gain in the Orange Bowl on January 1, 1971.

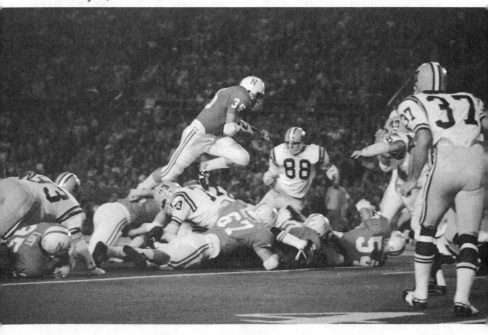

Jerry List grabs a pass in the Orange Bowl on January 1, 1971, against LSU defender Tommy Casanova (37).

After the victory, Devaney started politicking for the Cornhuskers, fearing that Notre Dame's impressive 24–11 victory over top-ranked Texas might vault the Fighting Irish even over Nebraska into the top spot in the Associated Press poll.

"Bob said, 'Even the pope wouldn't vote for Notre Dame,'" Walden recalled. "I thought, 'Oh my God.' God must have swayed the voting. The Cornhuskers wound up number one.

Another Title: Perfection

Nebraska entered the 1971 season as the number-two-ranked team in the country and would, eventually win a second-straight national title. The Cornhuskers would become the first team to go wire-to-wire as the Associated Press's number-one team in each regular-season weekly poll since the great Doc Blanchard and Glenn Davis Army team of 1945.

Before meeting Oklahoma in the "Game of the Century" on Thanksgiving Day of 1971, the Cornhuskers had outscored their first 10 opponents by an average of 38.9–6.4. Nebraska's closest game had been a 31–7 victory over Colorado, a team which would wind up third in the final Associated Press poll behind Nebraska and Oklahoma. In almost any other year, the Buffaloes might have won the national title.

Before meeting Nebraska, Oklahoma had mowed down nine straight opponents in fashioning an unbeaten record heading into this epic game at Owen Field. The Sooners had won by an average score of 45.0–16.2, and their closest game had been a 33–20 victory over Southern California.

It was OU's flamboyant wishbone with quarterback Jack Mildren at the controls and Greg Pruitt carrying the ball versus Jerry Tagge and Jeff Kinney doing the same in NU's I formation attack.

There were All–Big Eight Conference players galore in this game pitting the top two teams in college football, which had been on a collision course all season. Both teams had played on November 13, with Nebraska hammering Kansas State 44–17 in Manhattan, and Oklahoma overwhelming Kansas 56–10.

"We played our last game [against Kansas State], and we did not play until Thanksgiving," said Jim Walden, an NU assistant coach at the time. "The first three days we looked at film, we thought we could shut them down. The following week, we didn't know. The closer we got to the game, we knew how sensational they were playing."

There was a difference of opinion of just how the game would unfold. Both teams had spectacular defenses. Oklahoma certainly did not take a back seat in that department to Nebraska.

"We had some really good defensive players—Lucious Selmon and Derland Moore," said Jim Dickey, an assistant OU coach. "We knew when we went out there we would win by a big score."

Had Oklahoma run a conventional offense, Nebraska's outside linebackers or ends might have had an easier time, especially Willie Harper, who was a dynamic pass rusher. On the season, Nebraska would cause 47 turnovers (20 recovered fumbles and 27 interceptions).

There were seven All–Big 8 selections on Nebraska's 1971 defense: Willie Harper (end), Larry Jacobson (tackle), Rich Glover (middle guard), Bob Terrio (linebacker), Jim Anderson (back), Bill Kosch (back), Joe Blahak (back). Jacobson won the Outland Trophy (best interior lineman) in 1971 and Glover won it, along with the Lombardi, in 1972.

"They were great [defensive] players," said Walden. "Harper had so much speed. Those were the wishbone years. Willie Harper was such a great pass rusher, he was so quick. But in the wishbone (which OU ran), you don't ever play a pass. You sit, sit, sit, and go out and play the quarterback or pitch. He would have loved to play in this (current) era."

The only team to halfway slow down OU that season was Missouri. Al Onofrio, the defensive master who had become Missouri's head coach that season, had held OU to 20 points in a 17-point loss in Columbia. Otherwise, the OU games had been track meets.

"I had never known about hives or nerves," Walden said. "I distinctly remember, prior to the game, my fingers were splitting. My hands got so dry, I had to put Vaseline all over them. It was nerves, almost like hives. That's how it affected me. I was so nervous I couldn't breathe."

Sports Illustrated featured both teams on the cover, helmeted OU's Greg Pruitt and NU's Bob Terrio facing each other, with the headline: Irresistible Oklahoma Meets Immovable Nebraska. And with a national television audience on ABC watching, the atmosphere on a gray day in Norman was tense.

Since the Associated Press poll began in 1936, it was the 14th game to involve the number-one and -two teams in college football. And for the first time, the Big 8 Conference had two of its teams ranked first and second in a game. Although there had been two ties, only in one of the previous 13 games between the top two teams had been an upset. And this game followed the usual pattern.

This game had all the drama of Michigan State 10, Notre Dame 10 in 1966; Army 0, Notre Dame 0, 1946; and Texas 15, Arkansas 14 in 1969. But it wasn't clear until the very end NU would win.

Nationally, Nebraska ranked in the top five in scoring defense, rushing defense, and total defense. But it had to rely on its offense this day, which averaged 437.7 yards a game.

Osborne, then an assistant coach, later said the Cornhuskers didn't know how to defend the Sooners' wishbone, and Oklahoma, likewise, couldn't stop Nebraska's potent attack. "We pretty much just ran up and down the field," Osborne said.

Nebraska struck first when Johnny Rodgers scored on a 72-yard punt return with 11:28 remaining in the first quarter for a 7–0 lead. This was the granddaddy of all punt returns shown on television year after year.

"I thought John should have called for a fair catch," Devaney said at the time. "I am not sure it ever entered his mind."

Rodgers got out of a tackle by Pruitt and actually put a hand on the field to regain his balance. Although the Nebraska blocks in the front of him were to the right, Rodgers zigged when maybe he should have zagged. He went left through a maze of OU players. All the Sooners missed him. He beat OU punter Joe Wylie, who was knocked out of the way by Nebraska's Joe Blahak. "John could have crawled in after that," Devaney said.

"Even at that young age [of 11 years old], I knew that was a football game," said Darrell Ray Dickey, son of Jim and a ball boy for OU at the time and later the Kansas State quarterback. "And, yes, there were three clips on Johnny Rodgers's punt return....I saw them all, but what a great game!"

Father Jim, the OU assistant, said no one on the OU side could really gripe about it. Then came the seesaw of a game—back and forth, up and down, emotions on a roller coaster for an entire chilly afternoon. Jacobson said because of his nerves, his knees felt like rubber in the first quarter.

OU sliced Nebraska's lead to 7–3 on a field goal. Jeff Kinney scored on one-yard run for a 14–3 Nebraska edge. Oklahoma quarterback Jack Mildren matched that with a rushing score of his own and threw a 24-yard pass for a 17–14 halftime lead.

The second half was more of the same drama. Kinney, on his way to a four-touchdown afternoon, scored twice in the third quarter to put Nebraska up 28–17. Then it was Mildren's turn again, with a three-yard touchdown run with 28 seconds remaining in the third quarter. The score stood, Nebraska 28, Oklahoma 24 entering the fourth quarter.

And then Mildren passed 17 yards to Jon Harrison with 7:10 left for a 31–28 OU lead.

There was one more drive left in the Cornhuskers for an 11–0 record, heading into a regular-season-ending game at Hawaii, a bonus 12th game, and then a bowl, the Orange Bowl in Miami, Florida.

"What I remember most, we scored, and they came right back down and beat us. It was a game where they were really good and we were really good," Jim Dickey said. "They just beat us."

Tagge took Nebraska on a 74-yard drive for glory, much as he did the previous season in the Orange Bowl. Rodgers had a crucial 12-yard reception to keep the drive alive on a third-down play. Kinney ran the final two yards for a 35–31 victory with 1:38 remaining.

Oklahoma had one last-chance possession. But on third down, Mildren was sacked by Jacobson. And on fourth down, Glover batted down Mildren's pass. Game. Set. And Big Eight Championship with a chance for a second straight national championship.

"Larry Lacewell [who was an OU assistant coach] said it was the most crushing loss of his entire career year," Walden said. "It was a game of all-stars. You knew it was going to be something good because there were so many good players. I have always said the greatest team not to win a national championship was the

Johnny Rodgers dodged multiple Alabama defenders at the start of his 77-yard punt return in the first quarter of the Orange Bowl on January 1, 1972, to score Nebraska's second touchdown.

1971 Oklahoma team. It would have been a champion any other year. I have always said it was the most deserved team that didn't win the championship."

After a 45–3 dismantling of Hawaii in the Islands, Devaney had a score to settle with Bear Bryant in the Orange Bowl. The Ol' Bear had put the squeeze on Nebraska in the 1966 Orange Bowl, 39–28, and in the 1967 Sugar Bowl, 34–7. Those bowl losses had led Devaney to the misguided let's-lose-weight-to-get-faster experiment that resulted in two 6–4 seasons of 1967 and 1968. Devaney then implemented a weight-training program, and the Cornhuskers got big again, which led them to their current status.

For the second straight season, Nebraska would win a national championship in the Orange Bowl, and Tagge would be the game's Offensive MVP. Only this game was not close, despite the fact, oddly, that it was the second time in three games Nebraska had to defend its top ranking against the number-two team.

Nebraska jumped on second-ranked Alabama for a 14–0 lead first on a short run by Kinney and then on a 77-yard punt return by Rodgers on the final play of the first quarter. Nebraska added 14 more points in the second quarter on a couple of runs for a 28–0 halftime lead. The 38–6 rout was on in Miami. Glover also won his first of two Defensive MVP Orange Bowl Awards.

"The game was over by the middle of the second quarter," said Tagge. "That team had so much confidence because of Johnny Rodgers. Put him on the other side, and we lose."

The game ended Nebraska's season at 13–0 and left Bryant in awe of what he had just seen. After the game, Bryant called this Nebraska team, "one of the greatest, if not the greatest teams" he had ever seen. And no one could really disagree. There were no split votes for national champions this season.

chapter 5

Transitioning to Tom Osborne

Future Nebraska legend Tom Osborne took over at the start of the 1973 season.

Bob Devaney had indicated that the 1972 season would be his final season and Tom Osborne would be his replacement.

Devaney had a star-studded assistant coaching staff that year, with five assistants who would later be head coaches on the major-college level—Osborne (Nebraska), Warren Powers (Washington State, Missouri), Jim Walden (Washington State, Iowa State), Carl Selmer (Miami), and Monte Kiffin (North Carolina State). This would be their last season together, as Selmer, who many thought should have been the successor instead of Osborne, headed to Miami and took Walden with him.

The Cornhuskers entered the 1972 season with a 32-game unbeaten string, two straight national titles, a number-one ranking, the front-runner for the 1972 Heisman Trophy—superstar Johnny Rodgers—and the eventual Outland Trophy winner—Rich Glover. What the Cornhuskers didn't have was a sure-fire replacement for the departed seniors Jerry Tagge and Van Brownson at quarterback. And it showed in the season opener, a shocking 20–17 loss at UCLA.

The Cornhuskers had a quarterback derby between David Humm and Steve Runty, not a rotation.

"In the 1972 season opener, we lost to UCLA," Walden remembered. "Mark Harmon was the UCLA quarterback. He couldn't throw the ball. He wasn't a classic thrower. But Pepper Rodgers was running the wishbone. Harmon scored a couple of touchdowns off the bootleg. We were better. There was a controversy. David Humm didn't give us the best chance to win the game. We had a quarterback named Steve Runty who was better right then.

"I always thought we lost it because we didn't start him," Walden added. "There was a real dissension process at quarterback. David Humm was so highly regarded. We didn't play great offense in that game. Had Runty started and we had brought Humm in, I think we would have a better chance to win the game. But we started Dave Humm and brought Runty into the game."

Unranked UCLA forced Nebraska into five turnovers and kicked a field goal with 22 seconds remaining to beat the

Cornhuskers. A few days later, Devaney appeared before the Extra Point Club in Lincoln, and observed, "The coaching staff drew straws to see who would come down here, and I lost."

Nebraska had a perplexing 1972 season.

After the UCLA stunner, the Cornhuskers' defense and offense looked brilliant in shutouts against Minnesota (49–0), Missouri (62–0), Kansas (56–0), and Oklahoma State (34–0). And they boasted victories over Army (77–7), Texas A&M (37–7), and Colorado (33–10), before a 23–23 tie against Iowa State. Eight turnovers against the Cyclones were disastrous. Devaney told reporters after the game that he had never been so disgusted with a team

"Iowa State missed an extra point or they would have beaten us," Walden said of a game which basically cost Nebraska any shot at a third straight national title. Iowa State kicker Tom Goedjen missed the extra point with 23 seconds left after the Cyclones drove 74 yards in 35 seconds to tie the score.

In 1972 Nebraska won or shared its fourth straight Big Eight title despite a 17–14 loss to probation-riddled Oklahoma in the last regular-season game. It hardly lived up to the previous season's "Game of the Century," because Nebraska's Johnny Rodgers and Oklahoma's Greg Pruitt were bottled up by the opposition's defense in the 1972 game.

1970, 1972 Army Games Drove Devaney Nuts

In 1970 Nebraska was on the way to its first national title under Bob Devaney. But during a 28–0 victory over Army in the third game of the season, Nebraska led only 7–0 at halftime against a team that would win only one game that season.

"I never have heard a man scream at players like he did [in that game]," Walden said. "He would almost turn into a mad dog with anger. It might take him a while to get there....I told my guys, don't move, that he would strip you. He went on a 20-minute meltdown. He spent the whole halftime screaming at practice players and redshirts. He half threatened to fire us all. To say the least, we scored three touchdowns and won 28–0."

Two seasons later, Nebraska traveled to West Point for the return game. ABC had selected Army's season opener against the Cornhuskers for a regional telecast. And Devaney was particularly agitated that a perception would develop that Nebraska was running up the score during a 77–7 Nebraska victory that was seen by a large part of the country.

"We could only travel 50 to 55 guys," Walden said. "We have one of the finest teams in America and we can only take 50 guys. And we are so much better than they are. The score is 35–0 at half. He doesn't know what to say. He is half grousing. We kick off. They throw a pass. And Bill Sloey, a linebacker, intercepts it and runs into the end zone. I have four linebackers [on the trip] and one of my backups gets hurt. I have three players the entire second half. I start rotating them. He is screaming, walking up and down the sideline, saying, 'What are we doing, embarrassing the military?' He is so nervous about the military academy. He couldn't deal with it.

"He looked out there and Willie Harper [a starting linebacker] is out on the field. He grabs me by the coat. 'What the hell are you doing with Willie Harper in the game?' I told him, 'I don't have anybody else.' He told me to get him out of game. He said, 'Play with 10.' He just didn't want him in the game because he was a starter. He said, 'I will fire you!' The very next week I walked up to him, and I asked him: 'We are not playing Army in the future, are we?' He asked, 'Why?' 'You fired me twice in the Army game. And I'd just as soon not play them again.'"

Rich Glover: New Jersey Pipeline

Noseguard Rich Glover, a senior in 1972, became the second straight Cornhusker to win the Outland Trophy after Larry Jacobson in 1971. The 6'1", 235-pound middle guard not only won the Outland Trophy his senior year (1972), he finished third

Nebraska's all-everything back Johnny Rodgers poses with the Heisman Memorial Trophy he won in a landslide on December 5, 1972, in New York City.

in the Heisman Trophy voting behind teammate Johnny Rodgers and Oklahoma running back Greg Pruitt.

Glover's third-place finish in the Heisman Trophy balloting, going forward, was one of only four top-three finishes by a defensive player through the 2007 season. His senior season at Nebraska, Glover finished with 100 tackles (52 unassisted). Nine of the tackles resulted in 41 yards in losses. Nebraska led the Big Eight in total defense and ranked among the top 10 in the country in total defense, scoring defense, and pass defense.

Only one team scored more than 20 points on Nebraska during the 1972 season, and eight teams scored seven points or less.

"Glover was the greatest player pound for pound to play the position," Walden said. "He had great lower body strength. There was such a quickness about him, it was impossible to double him.

He wasn't a lightning-fast nose guard. He had great technique. The amazing thing about him was his lower body. He had big powerful legs. Most of his power was in his legs. He bounced off things."

Recruited out of Jersey City, New Jersey, Glover said he was swept off his feet by the recruiting of Bob Devaney, who also was recruiting tackle Daryl White from East Orange, New Jersey, and some other players from that state. White decided on the Cornhuskers, and Glover followed.

Glover said in *Sixty Years of the Outland Trophy* that Devaney and his mother both believed in the mantra: "Go to class and don't get in trouble with the police."

Glover heeded that advice. And by the time he finished at Nebraska, Glover had moved from tackle in 1970 to the nose guard position. Glover easily had enough lateral speed to cover the option, which was in vogue in those days

"If you zeroed in and watched him play every game, he was phenomenal," said Adrian Fiala, a Nebraska linebacker from 1967 to 1969 and later a color man on Nebraska football broadcasts. "For a guy undersized and [not] lightning quick, he played only two years in the NFL. I knew he would have problems in the NFL because he was in no-man's land. He wasn't big enough for the line and wasn't fast enough or quick enough to play linebacker in the NFL. But he and Tom Brahaney [center] at OU had some classic battles."

Glover played two seasons in the NFL, one each with the New York Giants and Philadelphia Eagles, and one in the World Football League with the Shreveport Steamer.

1973 Orange Bowl: Send Off for Devaney, Rodgers

Nebraska played in its third-straight Orange Bowl after the 1972 season with no chance at a national title after a late-season tie to Iowa State and a loss to Oklahoma. But the opponent was Notre

Dame. It was the first time the two storied programs had played since the 1948 season.

The Nebraska–Notre Dame series was storied from 1915 through 1925, but the 1948 game, a 44–13 Notre Dame victory, had left a bad taste in Cornhuskers mouths for nearly a quarter of a century. The 1948 Nebraska team was led by center-linebacker Tom Novak, a Cornhuskers legend.

"Here's the deal before the [1948] game," said Notre Dame lineman Bill Fischer, who won the Outland Trophy in 1948. "In the pregame warm-ups, there were four or five drunk guys in the stands yelling, 'You damn Catholics...you can stuff your rosary beads you know where. Your Blessed Mother will not help you today.'

"One of our players went up in the stands after them. He was a tough two-fisted fighter. A couple of cops went up in the stands and removed the fans.

"Tom Novak had spent spring training at Notre Dame in 1946, but he left when all the other guys came back [from World War II]. He went to Nebraska, but he still had a lot of friends on the Notre Dame team," Fischer said.

"Coach [Frank] Leahy picked up the spark before the game and lit the fire. He said the first guy to throw a punch in the game would never play for Notre Dame again. But he said after every touchdown, put the ball on the ground and point to the sky and thank the Blessed Mother.

"On the opening kickoff, nobody went for the ball. Everybody picked out a guy and flattened him. Leahy had lit the fire. After the game, Novak asked, "What the hell possessed you guys? We told him, and he said, 'We were victimized by the guys in the stands?'"

The 1973 Orange Bowl was hardly a brawl. It was a Nebraska celebration, a 40–6 Nebraska rout in Devaney's last game as head coach and Johnny Rodgers's final game as a college player. During Rodgers's three seasons, Nebraska compiled a 33–2–2 record. And the Cornhuskers became the first team to win three straight Orange Bowls.

"The Orange Bowl game was a tribute to Johnny Rodgers and Bob Devaney's career," Jim Walden said. "Beating Notre

Dame like that was a nice way to finish it. We knew it would never be the same again. You couldn't defense Rodgers. He would play tailback, wingback, and wide receiver. You couldn't find him to double him."

Rodgers put together a highlight film in one of the great all-around bowl performances in college football history. He accounted for five touchdowns in gaining the Most Outstanding Player honors—three by runs, one by a reception, and one by pass against the Fighting Irish.

"Most of his career he was wingback or slot back," Fiala said. "Then against Notre Dame in the Orange Bowl, he played running back, and had 81 yards rushing. And he threw a 52-yard touchdown pass to Frosty Anderson in the 1973 Orange Bowl. He was a great baseball player. He was a great basketball player."

Rodgers, who had a 77-yard punt return for a touchdown against Alabama in their 1972 Orange Bowl victory, thus accounted for six touchdowns in two Orange Bowl games.

"They were a better team, and they just destroyed us," Notre Dame coach Ara Parseghian said in *Fifty Years on the Fifty: The Orange Bowl Story*. "It was a rare occasion when our team was taken apart. In the 11 years I was there [at Notre Dame], there were only two or three occasions where I felt we were not competitive in a particular game or a particular half. That was one of them."

Devaney's Enduring Charm, Connection with the State

Devaney could charm farmers in rural, western Nebraska, rub elbows with businessmen in Omaha, and hit the bars with the boys in Valentine. He had a presence about him where he could make one feel he had known Devaney for years. At civic clubs, at banquets, in the high schools, he was a walking memory bank of names.

"In watching Bob over the years, as a recruit, as a player, and as a broadcaster, he carried that ability beyond the field," Fiala said. "The best story I can tell you: my wife's uncle is named Ed Ingram. And Ed kind of resembled Bob a little bit. Ed met Bob when Bob was recruiting me as a high school senior at Omaha Bishop Ryan in the spring of 1965. Uncle Ed was a huge, huge fan of Nebraska. He went to all the games, home and away. And two years after Coach Devaney recruited me, Ed happened to be at a function I was at, a football function. Devaney showed up, and he walked right up to Ed and said, 'Ed, how you doing?' This was after two years, and Coach Devaney had met him once.

"That's the kind of process Devaney had with people. He could remember people and then he could put them totally at ease with a story or something about family. I think his number-one attribute was that.

"Secondly, he had one of the most capable staffs that I think was ever assembled in college football," Fiala continued. "Everybody on that staff, I think, was very, very good. And not only that, they worked together very well. It is rare, indeed, where you see that sort of cohesion with coaching staffs. He surrounded himself with good people.

"After practice, he would pull us all together. Blow the whistle. And we would all come to the center of the practice field. He would have a story for us, something funny, or something that would peak our interest. At least once or twice a month he would say, "Fellas, we are all pulling together, and that is one thing to always remember, to have good people around you. Business and sports, your family, surround yourself with good people. And if you do that, you are always going to be successful."

Fiala said that is advice he has always remembered and usually followed.

"There have been two times in my life in the business world I didn't follow that advice. It didn't work out, and one of those times it about killed me," Fiala said. "Every time I had a problem, I could hear in the background, I could hear Devaney say, 'What the hell did you do that for?'"

Walden on Devaney's Remarkable Memory

When Jim Walden was quarterback for Devaney at Wyoming, the Cowboys were playing at Utah in 1959. Walden tells the story of what happened in that game.

"You [the college players] could legally play a parlay card," Walden said. "There were 20 games on it. We would parlay two or three teams. We would pool our money. We would never bet on ourselves to lose. Be we would bet on the parlay card."

Walden said the Cowboys were leading Utah and had recovered a fumble. Devaney called timeout and wanted Walden to keep the ball on the ground and run the clock.

"In comes the halfback, and he tells me to keep it on the ground," Walden said. "Our tackle says, 'Bullshit, we can't do that. We are an eight-point favorite.' All we know is we have a $10 bet and we need to score. On first down, we are going to throw. I know if this doesn't work, I will get kicked off the team. Everybody in the stadium thinks we will run it. We try this pass. I faked a pitch and faked a dive inside. I pulled it back and threw it. I lobbed a 50-yard touchdown pass. There is not a guy near our receiver. We win the game. That was 1959."

Walden said in 1973, he and Devaney were driving to Grand Island, Nebraska. "We didn't like him to drive because sometimes he became too competitive," Walden said. "Something came up about the 1959 team and Utah and how it was a heck of a team. Without even blinking, he almost instantly said, 'If that pass hadn't worked, I would run your ass back to Mississippi.' He had never mentioned it before. He had never said a word. He suffered with me. That's why they called me the Mississippi Gambler. He didn't scream about me breaking rules. It was more like, 'Hey, way to go.'"

Osborne Becomes Head Coach

The big uproar occurred when Devaney tabbed the young, lanky Tom Osborne as his successor instead of line coach Selmer, who had been a Nebraska assistant coach (since 1962) longer than Osborne had been. But Osborne, a full-time assistant since 1967, had been the offensive mind behind Devaney's teams over a six-year period and ultimately proved to be a great replacement for Devaney.

"Obviously, it was not a mistake to give it to Osborne," said Jim Dickey, a longtime assistant coach in the Big 8 and head coach at Kansas State from 1978 to 1985. "Most people in the coaching business thought Selmer was in line. A lot of coaches didn't think Devaney did him right. That is just life. It was one of those things that happened. Osborne was one of the great coaches. And Carl Selmer went to Miami."

Whether the hiring of Selmer as head coach would have sent the program in a different direction is just a matter of conjecture. Unquestionably, Devaney's loyalty to hiring Osborne from within the staff set up the next 30 years as a bastion of stability at Nebraska and one of the great runs in college football history for sustained success. Osborne retained Devaney's other assistants (with the exception of Walden): Cletus Fischer, Jim Ross, John Melton, Mike Corgan, Bill Myles, Monte Kiffin, and Warren Powers.

"Bob was as feisty and fiery and social as could be," Fiala said. "Tom was the epitome of stoicism. He was just a very stoic guy. He never got too rankled one way or another. You couldn't have had two more different people in terms of off the field. When Tom took over as head coach, number one, there were a lot of people who were totally surprised that Bob appointed him. The odds-on favorite to be the nominee was Carl Selmer, the offensive line coach. He was a very good guy and a very smart guy. He had an engineering degree. Very methodical and very detailed in what he did. The offensive line was usually very, very good, except in 1967 and 1968."

Despite Osborne's age of 36, his selection was somewhat understandable because Devaney had an understanding of the ties Osborne had to the state. Osborne had Nebraska roots as long as many of the state's cornfields. He was born in Hastings, Nebraska, on February 23, 1937, and had a standout athletic career in high school. He was the state's athlete of the year in 1959 at Hastings College. And he wound up with two advanced degrees at Nebraska in educational psychology, the latter which made him Dr. Tom Osborne.

Osborne would have an almost professorial, clinical approach to the game on offense, with a hint of derring-do when the need arose. He certainly was a 180-degree turn from the gregarious, charismatic Devaney in terms of temperament and his relationships with his staff and players.

"There is no one way to make it work," said Frank Solich, who played for Devaney in the 1960s, later coached under Osborne, and succeeded him as Nebraska's head coach in 1998. "You can have a personality like Bob Devaney and make it work. You can have a personality like Tom Osborne and make it work. So the real key is really to be yourself: to coach within your own personality and not just try to be someone else. But, saying that, I took a lot of things from both guys in terms of how they operated and tried to fit that with my personality in terms of how I coached."

"Early going it was tough," said Jim Walden. "Tom's personality took an adjustment for the players. In the early years, they didn't like Tom. They loved Bob. But Tom never wavered. He never tried to be the new Bob Devaney. Tom had a different faith. He expressed it. Bob allowed stags and golf outings. Tom was more of a hands-on football coach than Bob was. Bob let the coaches coach. Tom, on offense, coordinated and called the plays. Tom was more involved on offense. Bob was more involved with everything."

The 1973 Season: Osborne's Baptism

The UCLA rematch from the previous season was in Lincoln, and fourth-rated Nebraska overwhelmed the number-10 Bruins 40–13 and rose to a number-two ranking nationally. There was a seamless transition, or so it seemed, from Devaney to Osborne. The Cornhuskers rolled past number-14 North Carolina State 31–14 before a 20–16 escape in Lincoln against unranked Wisconsin.

Nebraska went on the road for the first time under Osborne and beat a poor Minnesota team 48–7. That set up a game against 12th-ranked and unbeaten Missouri in Columbia. Nebraska had beaten Missouri by a combined score of 98–0 (36–0 and 62–0) the previous two seasons. But this game would hardly resemble those bashings.

And Osborne, like Devaney 11 years before him, would suffer his first loss at Nebraska to Missouri.

Rodgers, of course, was gone. And Nebraska never did receive that late-game magic to beat these new-breed Tigers led by All-American defensive back and returner John Moseley. The Tigers scored a late touchdown to take a 13–6 lead after Nebraska's Randy Borg fumbled a punt at the Nebraska 4-yard line.

But quarterback Dave Humm then drove Nebraska 72 yards in four plays. His 22-yard strike to Ritch Bahe with a minute remaining brought Nebraska within one, 13–12. The daring Osborne elected to go for the victory, but Humm's pass was deflected at the line, and MU intercepted in the end zone to preserve the victory.

Nebraska defeated Kansas the next week 10–9, and then suffered a 17–17 tie at Oklahoma State. Suddenly, Nebraska was only 1–1–1 in the Big 8. Three victories in the final four games eased Nebraska into a second-place tie in the league, the first time since 1968 Nebraska didn't have at least a share of the Big 8 title. Following a 27–0 shutout loss to Oklahoma, Nebraska entered the Cotton Bowl game against Texas with an 8–2–1 record and ranked only 12th.

But in its second try, Nebraska won a Cotton Bowl 19–3 over Texas. The score was tied 3–3 at halftime.

"We were soundly defeated," Texas coach Darrell Royal said after the game. "There's no question about that. It was so one-sided, it's hard to go back and 'what if?' this one. If I had to pick a turning point, it would be the interception right after the half. We had a chance to take the lead before that. But after that, we could never get in close."

Instead of sticking with an ineffective Humm at quarterback, Osborne made a coaching move that proved pivotal in the second half and eased the stress of the season.

"There was nothing wrong with Humm," Osborne said. "But we had to get things going. [Steve] Runty's a senior, and we had confidence in him all along."

Runty directed Nebraska to two third-quarter scores, both on runs, as Nebraska emerged with a 16–3 lead and then tacked on a field goal in the final quarter.

"We expected more trouble from Texas, but you have gotta say this about them—they never quit," said Nebraska defensive tackle Daryl White. "As a senior, I wanted to go out as a winner, especially after Oklahoma. This could have been our best game."

chapter 6

Oklahoma Series Heating Up

Oklahoma head coach Chuck Fairbanks welcomes Nebraska head coach Bob Devaney to Norman, Oklahoma, on November 24, 1971, before a Thanksgiving Day game.

The Nebraska-Oklahoma series heated up after the arrival of Coach Bob Devaney in 1962. And a decision three years later to move the NU-OU game to Thanksgiving Day for television purposes elevated the series to even new heights.

NU-OU became a Thanksgiving weekend staple, as much as turkey and dressing and early Christmas shopping. Coaching names such as Bob Devaney, Tom Osborne, Chuck Fairbanks, and Barry Switzer made impressions on television viewers everywhere. Players such as Johnny Rodgers, Greg Pruitt, Billy Sims, and Jerry Tagge became household names because of the unique exposure—the NCAA college football television plan allowed for only a few games on television each weekend during the regular season.

Thus Nebraska-Oklahoma occupied a national spotlight on television at a time when there was no overlap of college games until the U.S. Supreme Court in 1984 declared the NCAA plan illegal. It truly was a remarkable recruiting advantage for the two programs. The Nebraska-Oklahoma game has continued to be on television or national cable for years after that at various times in November, but the emergence of the game was significant in the 1960s and 1970s.

From the time of the first national telecast in 1965—a game won by Nebraska 21–9 in Lincoln—through the 1977 season, the game was shown on national television on Thanksgiving or the weekend after nine times before the 1978 game was moved to November 11 for a national telecast. And in most cases the game had some bearing on the Big 8 title, if not serving as the unofficial title game between two teams deadlocked atop the league standings at the end of the season.

Oklahoma had dominated the old Big Seven under Coach Bud Wilkinson in the late 1940s and into the late 1950s. The Sooners won the 1962 Big 8 title, but Wilkinson's resignation to go into politics after the 1963 season signaled the end to the Sooners' singular dominance in the league and over Nebraska, as well.

Oklahoma had to share the title of top dog with the Cornhuskers, really, from that point forward until the league folded after the 1995 season and the Big 12 was formed, starting in 1996. From 1962 to 1995 either Oklahoma or Nebraska won or shared the Big 8 title outright with other teams or each other in all but two years. In 1989 and 1990 Colorado claimed outright titles. Nebraska had 20 outright or shared titles during that period. And OU had 15.

Devaney failed to get the better of the Sooners, going 5–6 against them during his 11-year run as coach. Nevertheless, he won or shared eight Big 8 titles during that span to lessen the blows of those head-to-head losses to OU. Oklahoma would probably have exchanged several of those wins for the 35–31 Game of the Century loss to the Cornhuskers in 1971 that cost the Sooners the national championship.

"For two years in a row it was really us and Nebraska," said Jim Dickey, an assistant coach at Oklahoma in the early 1970s. "How do you forget the 1-2-3 year of 1971 [when Nebraska, Oklahoma, and Colorado finished 1-2-3 in the country in the Associated Press poll]? Then we go out and lose to Colorado in the 1972 season [20–14]."

That was OU's only loss of the 1972 season, heading into the next-to-last game of the season at Nebraska. Oklahoma still had a chance to win the league title with a victory over the Cornhuskers in Lincoln.

"Right before we go to Nebraska we had a big meeting and we were told they have awarded Nebraska the Orange Bowl bid," Dickey recalled. "There weren't nearly as many bowls back then. I will never forget, we were told if we don't accept the Sugar Bowl, and even if we go up and beat them, if the Sugar Bowl already selects a team, we won't have any place to go."

So OU took the Sugar bid in hand and later beat Penn State 14–0 in New Orleans.

"We go up and beat Nebraska 17–14. I think people thought if we had waited, we would have gone to the Orange Bowl," Dickey added. "That was something that happened I always thought other people didn't understand. I think we got a little criticism. That was like admitting we can't beat Nebraska. We were really as good as they were."

Oklahoma receiver Tinker Owens starred, Nebraska had six turnovers, and OU won. Later OU had to forfeit three games because of an ineligible player, and Nebraska was awarded the Big 8 title that the Sooners otherwise would have won.

Tom Osborne's Early OU Curse

Nebraska coach Tom Osborne came under the most heat for his early failures against the Sooners. Promoted from assistant to head coach in 1973 after Bob Devaney retired, Osborne lost his first five games against Oklahoma from 1973 to 1977 by scores of 27–0, 28–14, 35–10, 20–17, and 38–7. During that span, the Sooners either won or tied for every Big 8 title and won national championships in 1974 and 1975.

Osborne's number-four Cornhuskers finally beat top-ranked Oklahoma 17–14 in 1978. But even then, Osborne could not enjoy it much. The next week Missouri upset Nebraska 35–31. With Oklahoma and Nebraska tied for the Big 8 title, the Orange Bowl rematched the teams on January 1 in Miami, where Oklahoma prevailed this time 31–24.

Oklahoma then won the next two regular-season games— 17–14 in 1979 and 21–17 in 1980—as Nebraska frittered away chances to win.

"There was all that 'Sooner Magic' stuff," said Adrian Fiala. "I frankly thought it was a bunch of B.S. Some people bought into that. Sometimes it looked like our guys were kind of out there waiting for it to happen versus playing though it and getting it done. I think for a few years, they thought, 'Hey, it's inevitable it is going to happen. It probably is going to happen.'"

The head coaches in the 1970s and through the 1980s stood in stark contrast.

Although he may have shown a different personality behind closed doors, Nebraska's Osborne appeared to be bedrock: staid, bland, and consistent. Oklahoma's Barry Switzer was quicksand: flamboyant, controversial, and unpredictable. Osborne was the grandson of a Nebraska Presbyterian minister. Switzer was the son of an Arkansas bootlegger, hence the title of his autobiography, *Bootlegger's Boy*. And thus the contrasts in the way the two programs were run.

Under Osborne, Nebraska's program was structured and closed off to the media to the point it reminded people of a fortress. Nebraska's players carried themselves with a certain rigidity, almost military-like. Oklahoma was the Lazy Q Ranch, always open. Players were allowed to display their individuality on and off the field. Interviews and quotes flowed out of Norman like lava. Nebraska's players were usually under lock and key.

The openness and lack of structure under Switzer may ultimately have been the OU football program's undoing in the late 1980s when discipline problems unraveled it. But the OU football team usually played looser under Switzer, regardless of who had the better talent.

"I remember Barry Switzer's famous line from his pregame speech, 'Dear God, don't let the best team win,'" Fiala said. "There was that mystique. Call it 'Sooner Magic,' call it mystique."

This "Sooner Magic" was never more evident than in a 1976 NU-OU game in Lincoln when Oklahoma pulled out a pulsating 20–17 win.

"When we did start beating Coach Osborne, we knew we had gotten into their heads," said Dean Blevins, a quarterback on that 1976 OU team. "Coach Switzer never talked negatively about Nebraska....He always held Nebraska in the greatest light. But he knew when the fourth quarter came around, he would say, 'Do you think they really think they can beat you? Hell no.' They didn't."

Blevins was a central figure in the 1976 game.

"It was the first thing that developed the magic, us being the underdogs and us still winning," said Blevins. "We had won two championships in the 1974 and 1975 seasons. My senior year we were down a little bit. We went to Nebraska, and they had Vince Ferragamo at quarterback and a lot of big names. They were good, better than us. It was a cold, blustery, wintry day, and Nebraska had the lead late in the game. I didn't come in until the very end of the game."

OU trailed 17–13 with 85 yards to score. So Switzer emptied his playbook. And OU needed a quarterback in the game who could pass. A halfback option pass from sophomore Woodie Shepard to split end Steve Rhodes covered 47 yards. But it came down to a third-and-20 play at the Cornhuskers' 34 for the play of the game. Ah, Sooner Magic.

"There was like a minute [44 seconds] to go in the ballgame," Blevins said. "It was one of those real clutch situations going into the wind, the most miserable conditions. The play was called 'left 3-17, stop, and lateral.' We had run it so many times in practice. I would look out and see coverage in the secondary. They had busted coverage. It was the only time they busted all day. They did it on one play."

Blevins threw a strike to Rhodes, who was split left. He caught it 10 yards down field, curled hook, and lateraled to halfback Elvis Peacock, who caught it in a full gallop. The Nebraska defenders went to tackle Rhodes, but Peacock, with 9.4 speed in the 100, took it down to the Nebraska 2-yard line before he was bumped out of bounds. On the next play, Peacock scored. And Oklahoma had a highly unlikely 20–17 victory.

"It went from incredibly loud to nothing," Blevins said. "That place was stunned, and nobody could believe it. Any time after that, it was referred to as Sooner Magic. It was born in that game. It was born on that play. It doesn't matter if I am walking around Lincoln or if I am in L.A. and I run into some avid Nebraska fan. They will hear my name and they will say, 'Oh, no.' They will tell me they were there and what the exact situation was."

"I think Oklahoma was extremely talented. And I think Nebraska was starting to come into its own," said Frank Solich. "But Oklahoma had so much speed and so much talent. In those games, I always thought Tom did a great job of coaching, putting our football team in position to have a chance in those games. But when you are up against that much talent, sometimes it just doesn't work. We struggled for a period of time there [against Oklahoma]. We struggled in bowl games for a time. But everybody hung in there. And he got that thing turned around."

Better Times vs. OU

Nebraska beat Oklahoma three straight times, from 1981 to 1983, during the era of the Triplets (Turner Gill, Mike Rozier, and Irving Fryar). But as the Barry Switzer era at OU came to close, he won four of his last five against Nebraska, from 1984 to 1988.

"I thought up and down the roster, OU had better team speed," said Pat Jones, who was head coach at Oklahoma State during that era. "It would be interesting to see how many defensive players went to the NFL. I would think OU had more. Oklahoma was deeper in skilled athletes."

But the 7–3 victory by Nebraska in 1988 in Norman showed how good the Nebraska Blackshirt defense could be. Led by Broderick Thomas, Nebraska limited Oklahoma's wishbone to just 98 yards rushing. Oklahoma moved past the Nebraska 25-yard line just once. Nebraska won the Big 8 title with a 7–0 record.

And it touched off a period when Nebraska would dominate and wipe out Sooner Magic.

As Switzer was forced out after the 1988 season because of problems off the field and NCAA violations, Oklahoma promoted assistant Gary Gibbs, who held on for six seasons before Howard Schnellenberger lasted one. Starting in 1988, Oklahoma lost seven of eight games to Nebraska through 1995, the final season of the Big 8 Conference and Schnellenberger's lone year as OU's head coach.

Then Nebraska won the first two games against OU in the new Big 12, 73–21 and 69–7 in the 1996 and 1997 seasons, respectively, when John Blake was the Sooners' head coach. Nebraska safety Mike Minter, from Lawton, Oklahoma, was 4–0 against the Sooners from 1993 to 1996, when his Cornhuskers faced three different OU head coaches.

"That's why they let me back in the state," Minter said, "because we beat up on them the four years I was there. I really fell in love with Nebraska when I was in third grade....I fell in love with Turner Gill. Being in third grade, I didn't understand a guy from Lawton, Oklahoma, shouldn't want to go to Nebraska. When I got into high school, it was an easy decision for me."

With the formation of the Big 12 in 1996, Nebraska was competing in the North Division of the league, and Oklahoma was in the South. Because of the rotation of opponents in crossover games between divisions, it meant there would be two-year gaps in regularly scheduled games between the two Big Reds. That was, unless, the teams scheduled a nonconference game in the two-year period when they weren't playing conference games.

"We wanted to play it every year, even on a nonconference basis," said Bill Byrne, Nebraska's athletics director at the time. "And we made that offer to Oklahoma. They weren't quite as interested as we were. They told us their rival was the University of Texas."

Down the Stretch

Thus Nebraska and Oklahoma didn't play in 1998 and 1999. Nebraska lost to Oklahoma 31–14 in 2000. That was one of two losses during the regular season for the 10–2 Cornhuskers. But in 2001 Oklahoma came to Lincoln as the number-two-ranked team in the country—and on a 20-game winning streak—to face number-three Nebraska. It was the highest the two teams had been ranked going into this rivalry game since number-one Nebraska lost to number-two Oklahoma 17–7 in 1987.

"Oklahoma had always been the rivalry game for Nebraska," said Nebraska's quarterback in 2001, Eric Crouch, the Cornhuskers' third Heisman Trophy winner. "I think that rivalry got lost because we were not playing every year [when the Big 12 was formed]. But, when Oklahoma came to town in 2001, they had won 20 straight games, and we were on a pretty good roll, too."

Nebraska head coach Frank Solich had pulled a page out of the Tom Osborne playbook—a trick play.

"To have that trick play was weird for me," Crouch remembered. "It was a one-shot deal. I remember we had worked on it all week in practice. On Monday before the game Coach Solich came in and showed us all the old Nebraska-Oklahoma match-ups—30 minutes of that—and all the trick plays that were involved in that. After he showed us the film, he raised up the screen, and here was this trick play on the board. And we were going to run it."

Crouch said Nebraska practiced the trick play all week, but it always got picked off or tipped, or a player would get sacked. Crouch would take the snap, throw it back to a backfield mate, and then become a receiver.

"I said, 'We better not call this play in a game,'" Crouch recalled. "'This is the worst play I have ever seen in my life.' Little did I know...he [Solich] surprised us all. We called timeout. And I came over to the sideline. This is after Oklahoma had tried the same, exact play, like, maybe a series or two before that—and it didn't work for them. He calls the play. I thought, 'You have to be kidding me.'

"I said, 'Okay, let's see if we can beat them.' And I didn't want to say anything because I didn't want people to know maybe we were confused, or something was going on and they would be tipped off to a trick play. I played like normal. I ran it. And it worked. It was amazing."

It went 63 yards for a touchdown to Crouch as the receiver. It was the back-breaking play in a 20–10 Nebraska victory.

Through the 2007 season, that is the only time that Nebraska has beaten Oklahoma in the new millennium, including a 21–7 loss in the 2006 Big 12 title game. Zac Taylor, Nebraska's starting quarterback in 2006, had been following the series since he was a kid living in Norman, Oklahoma. He had gone to Wake Forest and then junior college a season before he was picked up by Nebraska.

"Back then I was an OU fan cheering against Nebraska," Taylor said. "It always has been a respectful rivalry, not one with much hate. The 13–3 game in Gary Gibbs's last year [1994] was probably the first game I ever remember being at. Nebraska won that game. I definitely remember every game they have played over the last 15 years."

chapter 7
Missouri Series

Quarterback Scott Frost and Josh Heskew celebrate after Frost scored in overtime in Columbia, Missouri, on November 8, 1997, to win the game 45–38.

The Nebraska-Missouri rivalry heated up in the 1960s when coach Bob Devaney and the Tigers' coach, Dan Devine, had a series of contests that stimulated one of the hardest-hitting series in college football for a couple of decades. It was a series that was permeated by coaching associations and rivalries, border-state proximity, stinging injuries, controversy, and a general respect between the two programs.

Before Devaney arrived in Lincoln for the 1962 season, Devine's Tigers had shut out Nebraska four straight seasons by scores of 31–0, 9–0, 28–0, and 10–0. Devine won the initial coaching matchup with Devaney—16–7 in 1962—and in the process handed him his first defeat at Nebraska. But Devaney then won four straight over the Tigers and Devine, including 35–0 over MU in 1966.

A rivalry certainly was born then.

The competitive Devine detested getting beat by Devaney. The two were both assistant coaches on Biggie Munn's and then Duffy Daugherty's staffs at Michigan State in the early 1950s with other future head coaches such as Frank Kush, Bill Yeoman, and Sonny Grandelius. Devine, from Minnesota, and Devaney, from Michigan, were both from the Midwest. And they both coached hard-hitting, no-nonsense defense. Devine left the Michigan State staff to become the head coach at Arizona State in 1955, and Devaney eventually left to become the head football coach at Wyoming in 1957.

When Devaney and Devine both finally started coaching in the Big 8 in the early 1960s, the rivalry intensified between the coaches.

Wayne Duke, the Big 8 Commissioner from 1963 to 1971, remembers how Devaney would orchestrate the rivalry. In head-to-head meetings with Devine, Devaney prevailed only 5–4, but Devaney won or tied for six Big 8 titles to Devine's one from 1962 to 1970, when both were coaching in the conference.

"Bob used psychological warfare," Duke remembers. "Devine was outclassed by his psychological warfare. He would often outcoach and outsmart him. They had a rivalry going after OU fell off the top rung of the conference. Nebraska and Missouri came along and took over the reins of the conference. Devaney and Devine would have their tête-à-têtes. It always struck me as Bob coming out on top, as he was clever as hell." ·

With the Devaney-Devine coaching competition as a backdrop, the players began feeling the heat as well.

"Prior to my career, for years, Missouri has had that reputation of hitting hard," said Adrian Fiala. "Missouri people have been known as tough, 'show me,' and hard-nosed. Every player you talked to from Nebraska from the mid- and early 1950s on, the one game that was just the most difficult physically to play was Missouri. I think the 'show-me,' rock-bottom-heart mentality, was one thing. Secondly, Dan Devine was later the coach. He was a hard-nosed guy. He demanded that. So the translation to the field was such you better be out there hitting people as hard as you can or you are not going to play.

"We were the same with Bob Devaney. He demanded that. When you hit people, you just didn't come up and tackle a guy, you would tackle through him, so he wound up about 10 feet behind where he had been. If you do that, you hit people hard and you shake them loose a little bit. Nobody ever hit you as hard as Missouri did. I think what happened over the years, that perception and reality continued to build. Players every year would relate—and I am sure Missouri players would do the same thing—how hard a hitting game this would be."

Frank Solich agreed. "I would characterize the Missouri series as the most physical series during my time there at Nebraska," he said. "You always understood that probably was going to be the most physical football game you were going to play that year. It was obvious for some reason when the two teams lined up that it was extremely physical. And it always remained that way, regardless of who was favored or by how much a team was favored by. It was one of those games you just understood it was going to be an extremely physical game."

The 1965 Game: "Barnyard" Language

It is almost impossible to imagine that the 1965 Big 8 title was eventually decided on a penalty on Missouri's standout lineman Bruce Van Dyke for using "barnyard language" that official Glenn Bowles overheard during a crucial Nebraska drive in Columbia.

"I remember him having comments, 'horseshit' being used," said former Big 8 commissioner Duke. "Devaney had some funnies and was chortling about the call. It was a very crucial thing, of course. I do remember that the call was very important."

How important? The Big 8 title was won by the Cornhuskers (7–0), by a game over Missouri (6–1). And because of the penalty, Nebraska eventually was put in position for a late field goal in a 16–14 victory over the Tigers.

Van Dyke was flagged for his "manure" word, moving the ball 15 yards inside the 20 after a slow whistle and a ball carrier falling forward on a fourth-down at the Tigers' 34. Bowles heard the words of frustration from Van Dyke. And in the sequence of the actual play and penalty, Nebraska moved inside the 20. Eventually, Nebraska's Larry Wachholtz kicked a field goal from the 9 and wiped out MU's 14–13 lead. The NU victory eventually would send Nebraska to the Orange Bowl.

The next season, Nebraska bombed Missouri 35–0 in Lincoln. But then came three straight MU victories, from 1967 to 1969, including a 17–7 decision in 1969 that would send Missouri to the Orange Bowl for the final time in the 20th century.

"Nebraska was always hard-hitting," said Missouri's Sam Adams, who played for the Tigers from 1967 to 1969. "Nebraska was the first team to use weights in the Big 8. Our weight program consisted of a galvanized pipe and a two-pound coffee can with weights. We use isometrics, pushing against somebody. We weren't big, but we were quick. And from 1967 to 1969, we never lost a game to them."

The games still took a toll, remembers MU defensive back Dennis Poppe of the 1968 contest when he suffered three injuries in Lincoln. "Talk about a tough game....I suffered the broken arm, a jammed back, and hit jaw," Poppe said. "I could hardly swallow. I had to stand up on the airplane coming home."

Another MU player of that era said it was a clean game between the two teams.

"They'd fire out on you and try to beat you man-to-man, with very few tricks," Tom Stephenson said. "They are good sports and they are clean and they are hard. When the play is over, it is over. You get up and you look forward to the next collision."

Fiala remembers the intensity and the physical nature of the late 1960s games, including a 10–7 loss to Missouri in Columbia in 1967. He and future Wisconsin football coach and athletics director Barry Alvarez were Nebraska teammates in 1967.

"Nebraska never did beat Missouri when I played [1967–1969], but we had some knock-down, drag-out fights with them," Fiala said. "Barry was a couple of years older than I was, and he and I would watch film together. And we would pick up tendencies pretty quickly. We picked out a different alignment where Missouri was going to run Jon Staggers one way or another. And we saw how the linemen lined up. And so the first time they lined up the way we had seen in the film, sure enough it was Staggers. So we did a little check call, and I came flying through just about the time Staggers got the toss from the quarterback. The ball and I arrived about the same time.

"And I just separated him from the ball. And Barry was coming up from the other side from the inside. I was on the outside. And he was able to recover that fumble. And immediately when Barry recovered that fumble, he jumped up and was yelling over at me lying on the ground, 'Hey, do that again! Knock the hell out of him.' Some guys recover a fumble and it is all about them. But Barry was yelling at me, 'Great job! Way to go!' That's just the way he was.

"You wanted to make sure when you stuck somebody against Missouri, they stayed stuck," Fiala said. "I woke up after the Missouri game on Sunday morning, and I could hardly get out of bed. Always stiff and sore after a game, but never like Missouri. I think it had something to do with the fact that we were so psyched to play and you had such a great deal of adrenaline rushing through your body, it just exhausted your muscles, and you combined that with the fact it was a hard-hitting game. Sunday morning, you get up and you just can't hardly move."

The 1970s: Nebraska's Roller Coaster vs. MU

The decade of the 1970s would result in Nebraska holding a 6–4 edge over the Tigers. But after Nebraska won the first three games of the 1970s against Missouri under Bob Devaney by a combined score of 119–7, Tom Osborne was only 3–4 against the Tigers the rest of the decade. In all four losses, an upstart Missouri team beat a Nebraska team ranked fifth or higher.

In Osborne's first trip to Columbia as head coach, the unbeaten Tigers upset number-two Nebraska 13–12. Missouri's John Moseley had two long kickoff returns and a late-game interception that ultimately put Nebraska deep in its own territory, fielding a punt, which was fumbled. Missouri recovered at the Nebraska 4 and scored two plays later.

Later Osborne gambled on a two-point conversion play after the Cornhuskers scored to make it 13–12. But quarterback Dave Humm's pass was tipped on the conversion try and intercepted. That play sealed MU's upset victory.

Nebraska would not beat Missouri in Lincoln the rest of the decade. Missouri would register upsets there—21–10 in 1974, 34–24 in 1976, and finally 35–31 in 1978. Nebraska was ranked fifth, third, and second, respectively, when the Tigers beat the Cornhuskers at home during those years.

In the 1974 upset Missouri waited until 11:26 remaining and scored the final 21 points of the game.

In 1976 Pete Woods engineered the upset of the number-three Cornhuskers when the Tigers were 11-point underdogs. The previous season the Cornhuskers' had used a fake punt that turned into a momentum-changing and rambling 40-yard touchdown run by Cornhuskers lineman John O'Leary in Nebraska's 30–7 victory in Columbia.

The key play in the 1976 game was named the "Boomerooskey" by Missouri players because of the daring nature. Trailing 24–23 and fearful of getting a punt blocked in their own end zone (Nebraska had nearly blocked a previous one), the Tigers' coaches elected a long make-or-break pass from the Missouri 2.

Missouri quarterback Pete Woods completed a 98-yard pass to Joe Stewart, who was alone at the 35-yard line and took the ball in stride. Nebraska defensive back Larry Valasek came up and tried to keep up with him, but Stewart, from Evanston, Illinois, with 9.6 speed in the 100-yard dash, separated easily from him. Nebraska's defensive coordinator Monte Kiffin took the blame for the loss after the game: "Twenty-four points is enough to win. We can't give up the long bomb."

And in 1978 Missouri's James Wilder ran wild in the Tigers' 35–31 victory, which was probably the most bitter for the Cornhuskers because former Nebraska assistant coach and player Warren Powers walked into Lincoln a second straight year and beat his alma mater.

In 1977, in his only season at Washington State, Powers' Cougars shocked Nebraska 19–10 in Lincoln. That appeared to vault him into an even better job at Missouri the following season after the Tigers' hierarchy fired Al Onofrio.

"It was whisper-quiet when you walked out of there after the [Nebraska-Washington State] game," said Fiala, who was in the media by then. "But that was kind of like how Warren got it going. I remember this like yesterday, Warren was coming off the field, [after the game], I walked up to him. His face was like he had been in a tornado. He was in total shock. His eyes were big, like he didn't know where he was, quite frankly. So I walked up to him and said to Warren, 'Congratulations.' To this day I don't think he would remember me because he was in such shock over winning the ballgame. He was in as much shock as Huskers fans were in dealing with it."

Then, the next season, Missouri's 1978 victory over Nebraska came a week after Osborne beat OU 17–14, for the first time as head coach after five straight losses to the Sooners. Instead of winning the Big 8 Conference outright, Oklahoma tied Nebraska for first. And the Orange Bowl rematched the two league power-houses in Miami. OU prevailed 31–24 the second time in one of the more unusual turnarounds.

"Everybody is all excited about beating Oklahoma," Fiala remembers of the 10th game of the season. "I kept telling people not to get too happy about this because Missouri is coming to town the next week. They had [Kellen] Winslow, [James] Wilder, and Phil Bradley. They had a bunch of great players. I will never forget, after that, they announced that Nebraska and Oklahoma would meet again in the Orange Bowl, which really upset people. So Warren has had a hand in a lot of things."

The Nature of the Osborne-Powers Rivalry

After Powers graduated from Nebraska, he went on to play for the Oakland Raiders as a defensive back. But he returned to Lincoln in the springs during his professional football days and then as an assistant coach in 1969 under Bob Devaney.

"He used to come back every spring when he was with Oakland and work out with us," Fiala said. "He would work with us on footwork, game philosophy, and recognizing things."

Powers was an assistant for Devaney for four seasons and then stayed on another four seasons on Osborne's staff. Powers took the Washington State head-coaching job in Pullman, Washington, after the 1976 season.

Washington State just happened to be Nebraska's season opener in Lincoln in 1977. So Powers, right off the bat, was facing his alma mater.

"We did all the calisthenics before that game," said Mike Price, who was an assistant on Powers's staff at Washington State and would move with him to Missouri. "Our strength coach at Washington State was Dave Redding, who had been their assis-tant strength coach at Nebraska. We had all these former

Nebraska players as assistants at Washington State—Redding, Mark Heydorff, and Zaven Yaralian—and they eventually went off to Missouri. Nebraska had red tops with white bottoms and we [Washington State] had red bottom and white tops. We came out and spread out at the same time. We did Washington State spelled out, and they did Nebraska spelled out."

Given the similar colors of the uniforms and stretching form and techniques, it was confusing just which team was which.

"One of our players got in the stretching line of Nebraska in the pregame warm-ups," Price said with a chuckle. "And he started warming up with Nebraska. He was a freshman from Lewiston, Idaho. All the Nebraska players were laughing. And he didn't even know. The coach would make a call, and he would cross his legs. Our coaches got over there and got him out of there. We beat Nebraska in a thrilling game. Nebraska was not expecting that passing attack. We left the field after the game and got a standing ovation."

That victory set the stage for Powers to move to Missouri and then pull off the Tigers' 1978 upset in Lincoln. Little did anyone know Missouri would not beat Nebraska again until 2003 and would drop 24 straight games to the Cornhuskers.

Still, many of the NU-MU games were compelling during the Powers regime at Missouri, which ended in 1984.

In 1979 Nebraska's standout I-back Jarvis Redwine was injured by Missouri end Norman Goodman. Redwine was blocking on an extra point and took what Osborne believed was an unnecessary hit. Nebraska won 23–20 when Missouri tried to score a touchdown on the final play and failed. After Missouri's James Wilder fell down on a pass route, Missouri quarterback Phil Bradley was sacked on the play by Nebraska's Derrie Nelson.

"There was one play by one player that was so emphasized—Norman Goodman," Price said. "I kind of felt bad for Warren. He took a lot of heat for it. It was just one play. We ran [at Missouri] what Monte Kiffin and Warren had invented—the eagle defense—at Nebraska. Nebraska was still running it. Our offense was different. Lots of assistant coaches at Missouri then had played at

Nebraska. The flavor was thick with Nebraska people. That's going to happen. The longer you are going to play, the thinner the skin gets."

The 1980 game went to Nebraska, 38–16, in Lincoln. But the 1981 game was one of the classic defensive contests of the series.

Huskers Score in Final Seconds in 1981; Controversy Again in 1982

Nebraska was developing a high-powered offense in 1981 with Turner Gill, Mike Rozier, and Irving Fryar. But they were only sophomores. Going into the Missouri game, they had rolled Colorado and Kansas State by a combined score of 108–3. Gill had become the starting quarterback for the Cornhuskers during the season.

But Missouri was ranked 19th in the country entering the Nebraska game and would wind up in a bowl game for a fourth straight season under Powers. Nebraska won 6–0 on a three-yard run by fullback Phil Bates in the closing seconds on a bitterly cold day in late October in Columbia.

"It came down to one last series," Gill said. "It was a game in which they were blitzing a lot and had a good defensive scheme. But our defense played really well, too. Todd Brown broke a long one [to set up the winning touchdown]."

"Iowa was the best defense we played before this game," Osborne said of a 10–7 loss to the Hawkeyes in the season opener. "But Missouri is the best we have gone against now."

Near the end of the game, Nebraska went on a 10-play, 64-yard drive, taking 2:13 of the clock. Gill had pass completions of 24 and 21 yards, the latter to Brown, who took the ball to the Missouri 4. On third-and-goal from the 3, Bates scored.

"On the touchdown run, the coaches told me to stay off right," Bates said after the game. "It was a 34-trap. And I got good blocks from [center Dave] Rimington and [left guard] Mike

Mandelko. We showed our poise, and a last-second victory like this will build character."

That season Rimington won the first of two Outland Trophies, given to the best interior lineman in college football, and was the only player in the 20th century to win consecutive Outlands. But even on this day, he found Missouri's imposing Jerome Sally lined up opposite him.

"Their defense is one of the toughest in the league," Rimington said after the game. "But we persevered and came through in the end. Sally's a really good nose guard. He's got a lot of lateral movement, and I respect him."

"I think I had a hip pointer and I didn't play in the first half," Rozier said. "I went in and got a shot and played the rest of the game....Everyone was after us. We were the team to beat in the Big 8 back then. We had to be up for everybody."

Missouri running back Bobby Meyer rushed 37 yards to the Nebraska 34 early in the fourth quarter, but the drive stalled on fourth down, and the Tigers came away with zero points. Meyer nearly scored for the Tigers before being dragged down by the Cornhuskers' standout senior defensive end Jimmy Williams.

"I saw him break at least two tackles at the line of scrimmage, and I could see him out of the corner of my eye, so I just ran as fast as I could," Williams said after the game. "He was really hard to bring down the whole day. But we felt we have total control of the line of scrimmage. We found some weaknesses on the Missouri offensive line [during pregame preparation], which let us know we could keep constant pressure on the Missouri quarterback all day."

"The kids play their hearts out for 59 minutes," Powers said, "and then lose it in the last minute. It's really a hard thing to swallow. That's one of the tough lessons of life, I guess. They deserve better than that, but they didn't get it. And Nebraska deserved to win."

In 1982 came another controversial hit on Nebraska quarterback Turner Gill. Missouri defensive tackle Randy Jostes, a Nebraska native, was involved in this controversy, although much more of it was made by the Nebraska media than by either Gill or Osborne.

Jostes received threats from Nebraska fans and diehards after Nebraska's 23–19 victory in Lincoln.

Without Gill, Nebraska trailed 10–9 going into the fourth quarter and then scored two touchdowns—a one-yard run by fullback Mark Schellen with 4:46 remaining and a 16-yard run by reserve quarterback Bruce Mathison with 2:36 left—to pull it out.

"[Jostes's hit] was just a play they were running, and it caught me in a vulnerable spot," Gill said. "He hit me in the helmet, and he knocked me out. I didn't take it that way [as intentional]. It was nothing personal. [Powers] got his team really ready to play. It was two teams which were really ready to play and played physical."

Osborne said he didn't believe Missouri was a dirty football team. And the game's referee said Gill had his hands in front of himself carrying out the option fake and was just pushed down by Jostes.

When Jostes pushed him, Gill's head hit the turf, causing a concussion that kept him out of the rest of the game. Powers allowed reporters see the play on tape to make their own judgments the next week.

Nebraska's Domination Until the 1997 Classic

From 1984 though 1996, Missouri suffered through 13 straight losing seasons. Nebraska won every game of the series during those years. There were occasional close games, but the Big Red Machine usually rolled. Even in 1990, when the Tigers nearly upset eventual national champion Colorado in the famous Fifth Down game, Nebraska beat Missouri 69–21.

With the arrival of Larry Smith as Missouri's coach in the mid-1990s, the Tigers gradually improved. But it didn't show in the Nebraska series from 1994 to 1996, when Nebraska was winning two national championships. Nebraska cruised to wins—42–7 in 1994, 57–0 in 1995, and 51–7 in 1996—over the Tigers. But the 1997 game was totally different.

Nebraska, on its way to its third national title in four years, entered the MU game in 1997 ranked number one with an 8–0 record following a 69–7 victory over Oklahoma.

Missouri, unranked, was a 29-point underdog.

"Coach Osborne liked to go in and practice on the field. And this is what other teams do at Nebraska the day before the game," said offensive guard Aaron Taylor, who won the Outland Trophy in 1997 as a senior. "And so Coach Osborne wanted to get on the field for 20 to 30 minutes that Friday night. They said we couldn't get on the field because they were watering the field. The word was someone had left on the sprinklers, and they were drying it out with a helicopter. We ended up practicing on their soccer field that Friday. When we got to the stadium on Saturday, it felt like you were walking on a sponge. It really did.

"When you made your cut, you would tear up a one-by-one [square foot] or two-by-two piece of sod," Taylor added. "I remember vividly walking up to the line of scrimmage and going to put my hand down on the ground. Before I got set, I would pick up a huge piece of sod and roll it up. The sod would fold up when people made cuts. So I would unroll it and move it over so you would have some semblance of a field. We knew exactly why they did it [allowed the field to get saturated with water]. They wanted to control our speed. I could understand that."

Missouri took advantage of Nebraska's young secondary and held a 38–31 lead when Nebraska began the tying drive with 1:02 remaining in the game.

"It was a crazy game," said Nebraska's then junior I-back, Ahman Green. "There was no defense on the field on either side. Our defense was always highly ranked. That was one game it didn't matter how we were ranked, we couldn't stop Missouri's offense. We didn't think their offense would score that many points. It went back and forth."

Nebraska quarterback Scott Frost directed the Cornhuskers all the way down to the Missouri 12 with 14 seconds remaining in regulation. He threw an incomplete on second down. With seven seconds remaining, there was time for one more play.

"The main thing I remember is that Al Sterling [a Missouri player] intercepted a pass [on the last drive]," said MU linebacker Duke Revard, who was redshirted as a freshman and standing on the sideline. "They didn't give it to him. They said he trapped it. It would have ended the drive. That should have ended it. His hands were underneath it. We were in a prevent defense. I always hated prevent. That's the only defense people can pass on. If we had just stayed in a blitzing aggressive package, we could have shut them down [and won the game]."

As it was, Frost had Nebraska in position to tie the score when he spotted wingback Shevin Wiggins in the end zone. Wiggins was hit and dropped the ball, but somehow kicked it in the air. And a diving freshman, Matt Davison, was the recipient of the touchdown.

"I was on the field [for the tying TD]," said Green. "There was no blitz, but I stood in there in case anybody came in and put pressure on Scott. I've seen it over and over again. But at the time I didn't know [the ball] got kicked up in the air. I saw the ball pop up in the air and Matt Davison catch it. Great game."

"I remember I thought the game was over," Revard said. "The sprinklers went off, and fans started to crowd the field in our end. They thought we had won."

"I was on the field. I can remember making my block," Taylor added. "I remember the ball being in the air from Frost, and it was going to Wiggins. From my vantage point, it looked like it went off his chest. And then he was falling backwards and you see his leg come up and you see the ball. And I saw Matt Davison. All the linemen were tired, whether it was the Missouri Tigers or us. And then I see Matt give it the touchdown sign, and so that's what I did all the way back [to the sideline]. I was the second guy to put up the touchdown sign. Shoot, even if the ball hit the ground, you want to make them think it is a touchdown. It was kind of surreal."

Nebraska scored in its first possession of overtime when Frost went over on an option play. Missouri quarterback Corby Jones couldn't lead the Tigers into the end zone, and Nebraska emerged with a 45–38 overtime victory witnessed this time by a national television audience.

The game-ending play was a sack of Jones by two former Missouri high school players. Mike Rucker from St. Joseph, Missouri, came from one side, and Grant Wistrom from Webb City, the other.

Missouri running back T.J. Leon said later of the Nebraska series as it evolved into the new millennium: "They knew just how far to push it, plus they were Nebraska. It was almost like they were expected to win. They were expected to be able to get by with just enough. They were the dirtiest team we ever played. I think Osborne was a great coach. And I am not going to take away from his legacy or the athletes he recruited or who he chose to put on the field. But they knew just how far to push the line.

"Their mentality was, 'We are not only going to beat you, we are going to hurt you.' I think Mizzou had that mentality in the late 1990s. And you saw that with them bowling over people during that period."

With Brad Smith at quarterback, Missouri finally ended Nebraska's long winning steak over the Tigers in 2003 with a 41–24 victory in Columbia. The Tigers repeated that score in a 2005 triumph at Faurot Field. And in 2007 the Tigers, behind quarterback Chase Daniel, beat Nebraska 41–6 at Missouri. Certainly the rivalry was back, although Missouri has still not won in Lincoln since 1978, when Wilder had his big day.

chapter 8
Osborne's Legacy

Tom Osborne stands between Nebraska's two national championship trophies during a homecoming rally on January 3, 1996, in the Devaney Sports Center in Lincoln.

Tom Osborne's appearance suggested college professor, which he was at one time at the University of Nebraska while serving as a graduate assistant coach. The tall, lanky, redhead from Hastings, Nebraska, worked his way up to assistant and took over the Nebraska head-coaching reins in 1973, fashioning one of college football's top coaching records.

But the shadow cast by coach Bob Devaney's two national titles in 1970 an 1971 was long and deep. It took 23 more years before Osborne finally won a national title in 1994. Then he won two more, trumped Devaney's two titles, and retired from coaching after the 1997 season as his team won the third national title. Through the 2007 season, Osborne's 83.6 percent winning percentage ranks fifth all-time among those coaches who have 10 years or more in the NCAA Bowl Subdivision.

By the mid-1990s, Osborne had galvanized an entire state much as Bob Devaney had in the 1960s and early 1970s. Only his personality was much more reserved than the rollicking Devaney, who often was like a politician on the stump, hugging babies, drinking with the boys in Kearney, rubbing elbows with the state's politicians and businessmen, as well hob-knobbing with small farmers.

Devaney was as much at home with Warren Buffett as he was with Betty the beautician from Grand Island or Hank the trucker from North Platte. Osborne seldom showed anything to fans, media, or alumni. Maybe the only time that Osborne really opened up was in a game with his ever-present headset glued to his head, or on the practice field with his team.

So it was always hard to get a bead on Tom Osborne, who doesn't drink, doesn't cuss, and doesn't raise his voice often.

"He knew how to motivate us," said running back Ahman Green. "He knew the things he wanted us to do on and off the field, and we did them because he motivated us the right way. He had a real strong belief in God. That's how he coached. He didn't cuss a whole lot. He was a real quiet guy. A great guy."

The grandson of a Presbyterian minister, without a major-college playing background, Osborne, like Devaney, came up through the obscurity of small college sports at Hastings College in Nebraska. But he did play professionally two seasons as a wide receiver for the Washington Redskins. Ultimately, Osborne became the caretaker for one of college sports' greatest, most consistent programs of the 20th century.

He did it in a state that lacked population but had developed a system with a sophisticated weight program, redshirting, and walk-ons for the base. NU then recruited the legs and arms of the program, its skilled players, from both coasts and deep in the heart of Texas and other parts South.

In 25 seasons as Nebraska's head coach, Osborne compiled a 255–49–3 overall record, and went to 25 straight bowl games, including 17 straight "major" bowls. Through the 2007 season, only Florida State's Bobby Bowden had taken his team to more consecutive bowls–26. His Nebraska teams won nine or more games every season he coached and never lost more than three games in a season. His Cornhuskers teams won 13 league titles and six of the last seven seasons he coached. He was inducted into the College Football Hall of Fame in 1999, when the customary three-year waiting period was waived. The field at Memorial Stadium is named after Osborne.

Osborne's predecessor and mentor, Devaney was more of a CEO coach. Osborne was more of a hands-on coach, down to even calling the offensive plays as head coach. But they each showed that winning championships could be accomplished with a different management style and personality.

"Bob was outwardly humorous," said Frank Solich, who played for Devaney and was an assistant under Osborne. "You could see that humor almost all of the time. You could see it during practice. You could see it in meetings. The press couldn't see it. The people following the team couldn't see it. Tom had a sense of humor, but it was contained a little bit. You saw it in our staff meetings. I think the players saw Tom's humorous side on the football field. He and Mike Rozier would always go back and forth with jabs. He also had a personality where he could match up with players and get the most of them."

When the toughest decisions of both Devaney's and Osborne's careers arose, they either showed compassion or they compromised their standards when dealing with troubled players. Devaney allowed Johnny Rodgers back on the team. Osborne let Lawrence Phillips back on after a tough rehabilitation program. Each time, Nebraska won championships, although Rodgers's presence on the field certainly was more critical than Phillips's was.

Osborne's Early Head-Coaching Years

The Devaney years had been golden ones. Nebraska won or tied for the Big 8 championship the last four years he coached and won two national titles. The night of January 1, 1973, when Johnny Rodgers exploded in the Orange Bowl and Nebraska crushed Notre Dame at the end of a frustrating season, Devaney's retirement present was complete.

He handed over the keys to the car to Osborne the next day and slid over to the athletics director's chair. Osborne had a Lexus of a football program to drive and not a lot of insurance or assurances from the fans or alumni. His appointment was recommended by Devaney, so it stuck. But in his first season, there were questions about Osborne's play-calling inside the 10 as Nebraska barely beat Kansas 10–9 in Lincoln on homecoming. And some boos erupted in Memorial Stadium as the team trotted off the field.

Osborne told Hal Brown, sports editor of the *Lincoln Star*, during the 1973 season, "I've had people tell me they don't think the play-calling from the sidelines is as good as it was the past few years when Bob [Devaney] was doing it. The funny thing is the same guy [Osborne] is calling the plays."

But the Cornhuskers of 1973, with a league record of 4–2–1, failed to win the Big 8 title and finished in a tie with Kansas for second. And before they met Texas in the Cotton Bowl, Osborne also had to deal with unhappy cocaptains, All-American tackles John Dutton and Daryl White. They met with Osborne and discussed the team's unhappiness over his longer workouts, frequent scrimmaging (Devaney had limited scrimmages during the season), and practices running longer than even the stated time.

Osborne never wavered despite his stars' criticisms. Nebraska beat Texas 19–3.

Oklahoma quarterback Dean Blevins, who played against Osborne in the mid-1970s and later covered him in the media, said that was one of his keys to success. He didn't change because public opinion might be against him.

"Consistency—to the uniforms, packing stadiums, dedicated fans, the staff, the same coaches year after year," Blevins said. "There was a consistent message...his even-keeled personality. The way they went back out and practiced. They didn't alter their playbook much, we didn't think. They were able to get out and recruit with anyone. One thing is, consistency breeds consistency."

And winning at NU bred winning in the mid- and late 1970s, except against Blevins's Oklahoma Sooners.

As Alabama's Bear Bryant had been Devaney's tormentor with two crushing defeats of the Cornhuskers in the 1966 Orange Bowl and the 1967 Sugar Bowl, Barry Switzer was Osborne's. Osborne lost to Switzer five straight times before finally beating him in the 1978 regular season, only to lose to Switzer in an Orange Bowl rematch several weeks later.

Switzer would make headlines with his flashy quotes and similar lifestyle. Osborne was reclusive, even when it came to socializing with fellow coaches.

"Tom was hard for me to get to know," said Jim Dickey, who was an assistant on Chuck Fairbanks's staff at OU, later an assistant at Kansas and head coach at Kansas State. "He was a little more private. He was a very serious person. It was an event to get him to go get a cup of coffee. It seems like he was always going to a meeting. He was always on call. It seemed like he never had any fun. He probably was a tremendously good person. And I had tremendous respect for what he did."

But two more defeats to Oklahoma in 1979 (17–14) and 1980 (21–17) left Osborne with a 1–8 record against OU and only shared Big 8 titles with OU in 1975 and 1978. Osborne clearly was second-best in the Big 8 during his early coaching years.

Winning the Big 8, Trick Plays

In 1981 Nebraska won the first of four straight Big 8 titles, a streak that included three straight victories over the Sooners. A big part of that championship run was the promotion of Gill, then a sophomore, to the starting quarterback spot early in the 1981 season.

By this time, Osborne had developed the utmost internal respect from his players.

"He was very, very considerate, compassionate, and loyal," said Gill, who was later an assistant coach for Osborne. "He was a guy who was really there for the team and assistant coaches. He treated everybody the same. And when I say that, I am talking about whether you were the first-team quarterback or the fourth-team defensive tackle, he would treat you the same way. He would talk to you the same way, he would encourage you the same way. He was there for you—for your ups and downs, whether you were doing well on the field, off the field, academically, with your family. He was consistent in everything he did. There was no up and down with Tom Osborne.

"He reached out to every single young man. I saw it. As a player and as a coach. So that is why he was so beloved by people who played for him....That's why people played so hard for him. He wasn't a yeller or a screamer. He had a different kind of motivation. He also was a guy who talked to you about how to be the right person."

Still, it became a near obsession for Osborne to beat Oklahoma. It got to the point Osborne was resorting to trick plays. And they ultimately became one of the Osborne coaching trademarks in big games.

Against OU in 1979, quarterback Jeff Quinn left the ball underneath center Kelly Saalfeld. And 6'5", 232-pound offensive guard Randy Schleusener picked it up and ran 15 yards to score in a 17–14 loss to the Sooners. Even Gill was surprised to see Osborne put in a "bounce pass" for the OU game in 1982, which Nebraska won 28–24.

"I took the ball and bounced it," Gill said. "Irving Fryar caught the bounce pass and threw it to our tight end. You had to get a good bounce. Irving and I would kind of throw the pass out and made sure it would work [in practice]. We worked on it in practice, but it is nothing like doing it in a game. He had the 'Fumbleroosky,' fake field goals. He had trick plays here and there, and they all worked."

The "Bummeroosky" was one of Osborne's early versions of gadget plays in a 1975 game at Missouri. Nebraska had lost the previous two seasons to the Tigers. And Osborne, his Cornhuskers playing Missouri on national television, needed an early boost to get the partisan Tigers crowd out of the game. It was a fake punt. Fullback Tony Davis handed the ball to John O'Leary through O'Leary's legs. Nebraska's offense ran to its right, but O'Leary took off to the left and went 40 yards for a crushing touchdown.

"I think Tom was really good at coming up with things out of the ordinary. People look at his offense as the basic I," Frank Solich said. "But he had a lot of things coming off of it. I don't know that I would call them trick plays. Tom used to call them gingerbread plays. That really added to the offense."

Years later, the "Fumbleroosky" in the 1984 Orange Bowl, a 31–30 loss to Miami, was another stunner. Outland Trophy winner Dean Steinkuhler touched the ball to Gill's hands. He then placed it on the ground, making it a fumble. Any offensive player could advance it. Gill and the rest of the offense faked a sweep right. Steinkuhler pulled left and went 19 yards for a touchdown, which produced Nebraska's first points of the game.

But the play that seems to define Osborne came later in that same 1984 Orange Bowl when he went for two points and the national championship instead of a tie. The Cornhuskers moved within 31–30 after Jeff Smith's 24-yard run on fourth-and-eight with 48 seconds remaining in the game. And Nebraska came within inches of pulling off a great comeback from down 17–0 to the Hurricanes in their own stadium.

"About six inches on the pass from Turner Gill to Jeff Smith [for a national championship]," said Adrian Fiala. "If they kick it, they get a tie and they get at least a share, but Tom never played a game to tie."

After that game and those three seasons, Osborne still had not won a national championship. But his program was usually associated with the best in college football during his tenure.

"Nebraska was always very classy," said Darrell Dickey, who quarterbacked Kansas State from 1979 to 1982. "They lined up and kicked your ass, then went back to the huddle."

"People wanted to play Nebraska, they were so highly recognized," said Steve Hatchell, who was executive director of the Orange Bowl and later commissioner of the Big 12 Conference. "Anybody who would come in and play them would automatically be playing for the national championship. The road to the championship was through Nebraska."

"Every time we played Nebraska, they were the hardest hitting team," said Eddy Whitley, a Kansas State tight end. "Their linebackers and defensive backs were pretty physical. When you think of Tom Osborne, you think of very physical-type teams. Oklahoma was more finesse and speed. Nebraska was just strong and big and had wear-you-down type guys."

It was going to take some skilled players to add to this collection to push Nebraska to the national title level again.

Winning the National Title

Osborne's recruitment of quarterback Tommie Frazier from Bradenton, Florida, and Lawrence Phillips from West Covina, California—the hands and the feet of the program—pushed Nebraska over the top in its national title ambitions in 1994. The line, fullbacks, wide receivers, tight ends, and stout defense were already there. Nebraska still had its Jersey pipeline going. The walk-on program remained strong, basically with in-state kids.

"The basis of your team starts in state and then you complement those people with people out of state," Nebraska's future athletics director Steve Pederson said in a 1996 interview when he was director of operations for the football program. "A lot of the running backs have been Nebraska guys, from Keith Jones to Calvin Jones to Ahman Green to Damon Benning. Now, Lawrence Phillips is from California."

In 1993 Nebraska came close to Osborne's first national title when it lost to top-ranked Florida State 18–16 in the Orange Bowl. Frazier had Nebraska ahead, but a late FSU field goal doomed Nebraska, which missed a 45-yarder as time ran out. Frazier, however, had led Nebraska to an 11–1 season. And in 1994, despite the blood clot, he and second-string quarterback Brook Berringer would lead Nebraska to a 13–0 mark and the national title with a come-from-behind 24–17 victory over Miami in the Orange Bowl.

Osborne finally had won the big one. Frazier had been bothered with blood clots in his knee during the season, but made a triumphant return in the Orange Bowl. And Phillips led Nebraska with 1,722 yards rushing during the season.

With those two players and much of the rest of that team returning, and with the addition of other stellar recruits, including Omaha running back Ahman Green, Nebraska was in good position to repeat as national champions in 1995. And Nebraska would, with a 12–0 record. It would be, however, the most trying season of Osborne's career.

After the second game of the season, a 50–10 victory at Michigan State, the Phillips incident basically robbed Nebraska of its top running back for the regular season. Phillips was arrested and later convicted of assaulting former girlfriend Kate McEwen. He was suspended from the team, pending resolution of the matter. And Osborne was faced with a dilemma. What did he ultimately do with perhaps his best player, a discipline nightmare in his personal life, but a model player with extraordinary talent on the field?

Former Kansas State coach Jim Dickey knew what Devaney had done with Johnny Rodgers, who had been involved in a prankish gas station stick-up, more than two decades earlier.

"Under Devaney, Rodgers did crazy stuff," Dickey said. "I don't know if Tom would have put up with a lot of it. Devaney said, 'Boys will be boys.'" If Tom had taken the job a couple of years earlier, I don't know if Rodgers would have gotten back on the field."

Phillips got back for one game, the bowl game against Florida after he went through counseling and other rigors designed to cleanse his soul. But Osborne was criticized for allowing him back, as well as for other off-the-field disciplinary and legal issues involving other players during that time, such as wide receiver Riley Washington and linebacker Terrell Farley.

Through it all, Osborne remained rather unflappable, although he restricted access to his own availability to interviews as the national news media focused on the off-field problems.

"He's not a high and low guy," Pederson said in 1996 before the two-time defending champions took the field. "So in that way, I think it tends to keep your team from being a high and low team....I am sure he is tired. Like everybody else, it wears you down after a period of time. But he seems to hold up through all of it. If you feel like you have done the right thing and you have made the right decision, I am not sure what else you can do. I think he is a guy who will do the right thing, no matter what popular opinion is."

Moreover, his solidarity behind making a decision and sticking with it was admired by his players.

"I saw Coach Osborne get emotional when we were going through all the turmoil with our players off the field," said NU defensive back Mike Minter, who played from 1993 to 1996. "He was getting a lot of pressure outside. But he stuck to his guns. He felt like we needed to stick behind these guys, and I agreed with him. That was one time I saw him get emotional. I think it brought us closer together, because what we saw was a coach who wasn't going to sell his players down the river just because of what the media was saying or thinking. So it brought that much more respect to Coach Osborne. He was going to stick by his guys no matter what."

Osborne, who has written books on his coaching past and style, admits his inability to show emotion may come from his past, when he talked too much the summer before his sophomore year in high school and older teammates razzed him.

Devaney was just the opposite, even as athletics director.

When Marcus Dupree was a freshman at Oklahoma, and the Sooners played in Lincoln during the 1982 season, Dupree was 6'4", 235 pounds, ran 4.4, and was just rolling over Nebraska early in the game. Fiala was doing the *Bob Devaney Show* from the sideline.

"I basically asked Bob, 'Is there a danger bringing a freshman along too quickly [we had had some at Nebraska] and how do you keep them around four years?' He said, 'Well, Adrian, I just hope he flunks out!' Which blew everybody away, and there is still laughter. Bob could not exist in the world of political correctness. It would just not work."

Winding It Down

Osborne obviously coached in an era where he had to be politically correct, although he often outwardly appeared to be oblivious to what people thought.

"His public perception was that he was even-keeled, no emotion, dry, which honestly was quite the opposite of Coach Osborne," said Aaron Taylor, the 1997 Outland Trophy winner. "He was very good with individuals, whether you were a walk-on from out in western Nebraska or you were a five-star athlete. He knew you, he knew about you, he knew about your family. He is one of those guys who could say so much by saying so little. And he was probably the most intense guy out there. You knew when Coach Osborne was going to say something, it was going to be profound. And it usually was. He was not a much of yeller or a screamer, but he would definitely do that.

"We would always laugh if there happened to be a fight during practice. Coach Osborne would know the fight was going on, but

Tom Osborne motions to his team during his final season as Nebraska's head coach.

he would almost turn his back for about 30 seconds and act like it never happened. And then turn around and say, 'We don't need that out here!' He just was an intense guy. You could see the fire in his eyes. But he wanted to just play it cool.

"I want to say it was Kansas. And I can't remember if it was 1994 or 1995. And the game was pretty darn tight. I can't remember all the specifics because I was such a young guy. And it was the only time I saw Coach Osborne get crazy, say something a little different than his usual. He basically came back and told us we were playing like shit. And that is exactly what he said. That was the first and only time I heard him use language that was not Osborne-like. It was halftime, and everybody was, 'Uh-oh, he is not happy'. We knew we were going to win the ballgame. We were just worried what kind of practice we were going to have the following week."

NU kicker Kris Brown, who played from 1995 to 1998, added, "Coach Osborne has had a bigger influence on my life, other than my parents, than anybody else. What he stood for, what he believed, the things he tried to teach us about life off the field, how he carried himself. For me it was a very rewarding experience. Coach Osborne did a good job of making everybody on that team feel important. Not that they were just important to him and the program. They were important to him as people."

In the 1997 season, Osborne's last, he was the model of coolness on the sideline of the Missouri game. Trailing 38–31 in the final minutes, the top-ranked Cornhuskers were frantically trying to catch Missouri, which they eventually did.

"I never had a sense we were going to lose the game," Taylor said. "I don't know why. We had about two minutes to move the ball down the field. Of course, we were not a throwing team.

"I remember this vividly, we were standing on the sideline. And we called a timeout. And Osborne stood on the sideline so stoic. He looked at all of us and said, 'Guys, we have X amount of yards to go. We are going to run [these plays]. And linemen, I want you to make good blocks. And Scott [Frost], you make a good throw. Receivers catch the ball and get out of bounds. We will be just fine. Let's go.' There was no inflection in his voice that you made you think that it wasn't going to be that way.

"The fans were going crazy. There was stuff being thrown around on the field. I think it was oranges—frozen at that. As a young guy, you have so much adrenaline flowing through you, you feel like you could rip everybody's head off. And you come over to the sideline and here is Coach Osborne. He is very calm, very smooth and telling you everything is going to be okay. 'Make sure you do this, this, and this, you will be okay.'"

They were. Nebraska scored on that drive and went on to win 45–38 in overtime. They were on their way to a third national title in four years.

One of the most remarkable statistics during the Tom Osborne era was that Nebraska didn't normally lose to a team with a losing record. In fact, 4-7 Iowa State in the 1992 season was the only team that had a losing record at the end of season to beat Osborne during his 25 years as head coach. In the previous two games before meeting the Cyclones, Nebraska had outscored Colorado and Kansas by a combined score of 101–14.

"I always laugh and tell Tom to this day when we beat them [19–10], Tom's problem was he can't win the little ones," said Jim Walden, the former Nebraska assistant under Bob Devaney who was Iowa State's head coach in 1992. "He lost to one team which had a losing record—one team. I am sorry about that part. But what it tells you—it summed up Tom Osborne. He lost one game in 25 years to a team with a losing record."

chapter 9

Offensively Good,
Then Great Triplets

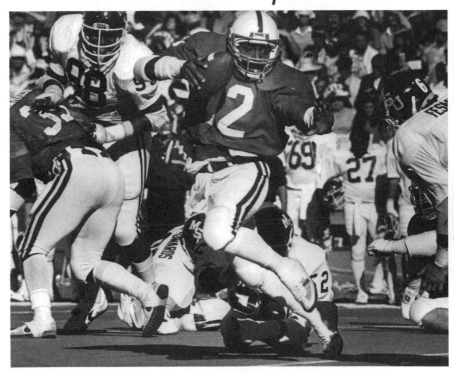

*Jarvis Redwine strikes a
classic pose as he runs
for 12 yards against
Mississippi State in
Nebraska's 31–17 victory
at the 1980 Sun Bowl in
El Paso, Texas.*

From 1973 to 1980, Tom Osborne's first eight years as head coach, the Cornhuskers only tied for two Big 8 Conference titles with Oklahoma, in 1975 and 1978. Despite a precision offense with big offensive lines, great I-backs and tight ends, and solid quarterbacks, they could never beat the Sooners, who won or tied for eight-straight league crowns.

The gaggle of Nebraska I-backs during that era included Monte Anthony (1974 to 1977), I.M. Hipp (1977 to 1979), Rick Berns (1976 to 1978), and Jarvis Redwine (1979 to 1980). Of those backs, Redwine, from Inglewood, California, probably caused the biggest stir off and on the field.

"Jarvis Redwine was an exciting runner, who could really run, and he had some long, exciting runs at Nebraska," said Adrian Fiala, former NU player and current-day broadcaster. "From a sheer excitement standpoint, he gave a lot of people a lot of thrills."

In 1979 Redwine posted the first of two 1,000-yard rushing seasons (1,042 yards), scored eight touchdowns, and averaged seven yards a carry for the Cornhuskers. That year they won their first 10 games of the season and rose to a number-three national ranking before back-to-back 17–14 losses–to Big 8 champion Oklahoma in the regular-season finale and to Houston in the New Year's Day Cotton Bowl–leaving Nebraska with a 10–2 record and a number-nine ranking. The loss to Houston was excruciating in the Cotton Bowl and signified how close Nebraska was in breaking through to the Promised Land.

Nebraska quarterback Jeff Quinn, with 3:56 remaining in the game, passed six yards to Jeff Finn for the score and a 14–10 Nebraska lead.

But Houston's junior reserve quarterback, Terry Elston, fired a six-yard touchdown pass to Eric Herring with 12 seconds remaining to win the game on fourth-and-one at the Nebraska 6.

"I thought the way the defenses had been playing, that 14–10 would be enough," Quinn said. "But Houston came back. And I give them credit. We were just six points away from being national champs."

Redwine: Heisman Candidate, Exploited Athlete

Redwine entered the 1980 season as a bona fide Heisman Trophy candidate and also with a few things to say to the media. The annual Big 8 Skywriters Tour rolled into Lincoln in August 1980, and the then-23-year-old Redwine, who had transferred from Oregon State to NU, basically blasted Nebraska and the NCAA for exploitation of the student-athlete.

"Football, to me, is a job," said Redwine, who was a married football player. "But I am not getting paid for it. Besides my scholarship [which includes basic tuition and books], I'm getting only $158 to live off campus as a married student. Don't get me wrong. Every time I go out and do something, I'm always going to give it 100 percent. I am always going to do the job. But when I need bills to be paid and I have to go to school, it is discouraging.

"I think all college athletes are exploited to an extent," Redwine continued. "But with standing-room crowds at Nebraska, I would think, if you are married, you could get more money."

An unauthorized poster of Redwine showed up in Lincoln during the 1979 season, but neither Redwine nor Nebraska saw any of the profits. Osborne acknowledged that Redwine was Nebraska's meal ticket to a possible national title.

"He's not an inside runner, but you sure don't want to let him go outside," Oklahoma defensive back Bud Hebert said.

"I am not one to pump up a player for the Heisman," Osborne said of the 5'11", 203 pounder. "But I have only been around one other back with the talent of Jarvis, and that was Johnny Rodgers. Jarvis is the finest running back I've seen at Nebraska in the 18 years I have been here."

Through the first three games of the 1980 season, Redwine led the nation in scoring and rushing yards per game. Game four, a stinging 18–14 home loss to Florida State, dropped Nebraska from third to 10th and also hurt Redwine's chances for the Heisman, which eventually went to South Carolina running back George Rogers. Nebraska won its next six games after the loss to the Seminoles, and Redwine rushed for 1,119 yards, nine touchdowns, and a 7.2-yards-per-carry average. But another loss to the Sooners at the end of the season dropped the Cornhuskers into second place and a berth in the Sun Bowl, where they beat Mississippi State 31–17 and finished seventh in the Associated Press Poll.

Recruitment of Fryar, Rozier, and Gill

Frank Solich was on the Nebraska coaching staff as an assistant when he was assigned the area of New Jersey as one of his recruiting areas. Solich had been a high school head coach at Lincoln Southeast High from 1968 to 1979, then moved to the Huskers staff as the freshman coach. He later was the NU running backs coach (from 1983 to 1997) before becoming head coach in 1998.

"They had been in New Jersey prior to my getting on the staff," Solich said. "So there was a history of getting players from New Jersey. And there were contacts there. But New Jersey was my first recruiting experience. I had come out of high school coaching. I wasn't familiar with being on the road. I hadn't even taken a draw [for expenses] to get on the road. I kind of had the feeling maybe I was given New Jersey because I was the low man on the totem pole. After I got to New Jersey, I started traveling around and found out you could see the school, you just couldn't get to it."

Solich said he got so frustrated at one point after problems with a rental car and directions to a recruit's school that he believed he might not be cut out for recruiting.

"I did not realize this [New Jersey] is about tough as it is to get around," Solich recounted. "I just kept plugging away. And I really got to the point where I was recruiting a lot of the East Coast, but always would start off in New Jersey. There was a time when we did have two guys. Gene Huey and I broke up New Jersey. He would take the north, and I would take the south, but there was a lot of the time I would have the entire state.

"Mike Rozier and Irving Fryar, in fact, were my first two recruits."

And Solich said Nebraska wound up with Rozier and Fryar by lucky accidents.

"I was at another school in the Camden area," Solich said. "I was looking at a tight end on the list, and Mike was on the opposing team and just making big play after big play, running out of the wishbone offense in the fullback spot. So I went over to that school and started recruiting Mike and ended up getting him. He wasn't as highly recruited as you might have thought and had to go to junior college. We continued to recruit him, and there was one school which came in very hard and was very close to home and you worried about if the closeness would become a factor. But he stayed very loyal to us."

"I went to [community college in] Coffeyville, Kansas, my first year," Rozier said. "I caught a Trailways Bus, and it took me a day and a half to get [to Lincoln]. Coffeyville prepared me for Lincoln. I knew if I could do Coffeyville, I could do Lincoln. I could have gone anywhere else in the nation. Once I got my grades up, everybody came after me. But Nebraska treated me as a person, not just a player. Plus, they featured I-backs, and that's a reason I went there."

Solich didn't actually see much of Fryar, who potentially would be one the last signees for Nebraska and turn into a wingback at NU. Solich went to the high school coach's house to watch film on Fryar, who was from Mt. Holly, New Jersey, one night.

"Fryar was playing tight end and safety," Solich said. "It wasn't like he was playing running back or was a wide receiver and catching a ton of passes. But you could see his speed now. He intercepted the ball at the safety spot and took off down the sideline. And I said to myself, I really liked this guy. He has great speed and he has a great frame. So I called back and they said to send some tape and they would take a look at him. This was toward the end— I think maybe Arizona or another school or two were after him. He ended up being a number-one draft pick in the NFL. Mike ended up going to the United States Football League. I happened on both of them by happenstance."

Future Husker legends Mike Rozier (above) and Irving Fryar were assistant coach Frank Solich's first recruits at Nebraska.

Rozier added, "Irving and I grew up together; Irving was my grandmother's neighbor. That's one of the reasons I went to Nebraska, because we had got together and talked about doing that. Unfortunately, I had to go to junior college my first year and get my grades up to go to Nebraska."

The third triplet, Gill, the quarterback, came from the heart of Texas. His recruitment came down to Oklahoma and Nebraska. And he chose Nebraska, which he led past Oklahoma his junior and senior years after being hurt as a sophomore.

"Coming out of high school, my dream was to be a baseball player," Gill said. "I felt my best opportunity to play professionally was in baseball. And I was drafted by the Chicago White Sox. I decided to go to Nebraska. But I didn't dream I would have the career I had in football [at Nebraska]. I wanted to play college football because I enjoyed the pageantry. But, of course, that all changed when I got there."

Pat Jones, an Oklahoma State assistant then and head coach of the Cowboys, remembers seeing Fryar as a freshman before he ever became one of the famed triplets.

"They would play guys as freshmen and then redshirt them a second year into that cycle," Jones said. "We used to play their J.V.s. Dave Wannstedt [another Oklahoma State assistant] and I were watching the Nebraska freshmen coming down the ramp. They had good-looking kids. We had this mimeographed program. And we saw this great-looking kid coming down the ramp, No 27. And it was Irving Fryar. He was playing on their freshman team."

The Triplets Coming Together

Gill remembers exactly how the 1981 season unfolded for him as an aspiring sophomore quarterback. Nebraska started the season 1–2, with a 10–7 road loss at Iowa, a 34–14 home victory over Florida State, and then a 30–24 home loss to Penn State.

"Entering the season, Tom Osborne said I was the third-team quarterback," Gill said. "Really, I thought I should have been the second-team guy. The first game against Iowa, the starter didn't play well. And we changed starters in the second game against Florida State. And he promised me I would play the first series of the second quarter. I went in and played four plays, and on the fourth play I fumbled. I didn't play the rest of the game. I thought maybe my situation was over [because he didn't play me the next week against Penn State]."

In the fourth game against Auburn, at halftime of a close game, Osborne told Gill he would start the second half. Nebraska wound up winning 17–3. Then the next week Gill started in a 59–0 victory over Colorado and was on his way.

That 1981 season I-back Roger Craig was Nebraska's third-straight 1,000-yard rusher. But Mike Rozier, as a sophomore, led the Cornhuskers in kickoff return average (32.4 yards a return); Fryar led the team in punt returns, (13.3 yards a return); and Gill was the leading passer with 619 yards and nine touchdowns.

The 1981 Cornhuskers, with the quarterback situation settled, won their final eight regular-season games, with only a 6–0 victory over Missouri being close. They won their first undisputed Big 8 title under Osborne after two first-place ties with Oklahoma (in 1975 and 1978). Nebraska's offense was becoming prolific.

"They run more plays and make more yards than anyone in the country," said Jimmy Johnson, coach of Oklahoma State from 1979 to 1983. "I am sure they had to pay extra postage when they sent their offensive film to us."

After a 22–15 loss to eventual national champion Clemson in the 1982 Orange Bowl, Gill said the Huskers' offense really came of age.

"Our junior year in 1982, Roger Craig was there. We had a lot of talent—Irving Fryar, Jamie Williams was playing tight end, Dean Steinkuhler and Dave Rimington were on the line," Gill said in noting the Cornhuskers' galaxy of stars.

And Nebraska might well have won the national championship in 1982 had it not been for a bad call in the 27–24 loss at Penn State, Nebraska's only loss in an otherwise perfect year. Penn State wound up winning the national title instead with one later loss. Nebraska, 12–1 after a 21–20 victory over LSU in the Orange Bowl, finished third in the AP poll.

"Every time I meet a Nebraska fan, they bring up the Mike McCloskey catch," said former Penn State quarterback Todd Blackledge. "That was a classic game. We led the whole game until the last two minutes. And they scored to take the lead. We got the ball back with 90 seconds left. We went down the field and converted on fourth down. And the pass to McCloskey on the sideline, it was questionable, he tried to drag his foot [in bounds], but it stopped the clock. Then a couple of plays later, we hit the touchdown pass to the other tight end, and that was a clean catch. It was not a great throw, but he did scoop that one and get his hands underneath it."

Replays showed that McCloskey was out of bounds

"An official was right there looking at it," Osborne said. "I can understand. We had our chances to win the game earlier. People tend to remember the last drive of the game."

Irving Fryar joined his boyhood friend from New Jersey, Mike Rozier, at Nebraska.

Nebraska scored 40 or more points eight times during the 1982 season. Besides the bowl game versus LSU, the only other two close regular-season victories were over Missouri and Oklahoma, both four-pointers.

"In 1982 and 1983 by the fourth quarter we were blowing everyone out," Rozier said. "You might get us the first two quarters, or maybe into the third quarter. But in the fourth quarter you were beat up and tired. We would just grind and grind and grind. Fourth quarter, we were in good condition and we'd just keep on going."

In 1982 and 1983 Nebraska led the nation in scoring and rushing. The Cornhuskers rushed for 394.3 yards a game in 1982 and scored at a 41.1-points-per-game clip. That was good. But the 1983 team was even better. It rushed for a nation's best 401.7 yards a game and scored college football's best, 52 points a game.

Fitting Together Perfectly

"All my front-line guys went first-round, and they were all corn-fed, all from Nebraska," Rozier said. "Back in the day, the line was from Nebraska, and the skill players were from Texas and New Jersey."

Center Dave Rimington was a first-round selection in 1983 by the Cincinnati Bengals, and tackle Dean Steinkuhler was a first-round pick by the Houston Oilers the following year. From 1981 to 1983, Nebraska won three straight Outland Trophies, with Rimington being the only player to claim back-to-back Outlands (1981 and 1982) in the history of the award that dates to 1946. Steinkuhler won the Outland as a senior in 1983.

"Rimington was just a physical player," Solich said. "Obviously he was a great center for Nebraska and one of the best of all time. He just had he ability to do it all at center. He had a very quick snap. He sometimes almost anticipated the cadence a little bit, but he was able to get it off the ball. Dean was probably one of the most physical linemen Nebraska had coming through that era. And he had the ability to pull and was athletic at it. He has a son right now at Nebraska who I think will be very, very good. He was talented with great strength."

"I remember one Friday in Stillwater before a home game against Nebraska, Rimington came out in shorts and a T-shirt and he literally looked like a Brahma Bull," Oklahoma State's Pat Jones said. "He was so compact and so athletic looking, we knew he might be a dominant center. Steinkuhler could really run. He was a better runner. He was a different type of athlete."

By the 1983 season, there was a poster at Nebraska titled, "The Scoring Explosion," and the stars were Rozier, Gill, and Fryar.

"The thing I liked about that team, as talented as it was on offense, those guys played together so well," Solich said. "Mike Rozier, in the Minnesota game [an 84–13 Nebraska victory], I don't think he might have gotten more than 12 touches in that game, and yet he is in line for the Heisman Trophy for the best player in the country and ready to set all kinds of records.

"I said, 'Mike, you got only 12 carries?' He was fine with it. You put somebody in for Mike, he was fine with it. Turner had all that ability and was throwing touchdown passes, and he was throwing to Mike a lot. And Irving was such a great receiver that he could have continually set records. But there is only one ball. Their willingness to work together for the betterment of the team made that team great."

And there was only one Heisman Trophy, which Rozier would win in 1983, when he rushed for a nation's-best 179 yards a game. He rushed for 2,148 yards as a senior, with 11 straight 100-yard regular-season rushing games. He was also an efficient back near the goal line, leading the country in scoring with 14.5 points a game in 1983.

By the time his three-year career at Nebraska was over, Rozier had rushed for more than 100 yards in a Cornhuskers-record 26 games, including seven games of 200 or more yards. Through the 2007 season, he was still Nebraska's all-time leading rusher with 4,780 yards, and he did all that in just three seasons.

"Rozier was a team player," Gill said. "And he had all the intangibles a great running back has. He had speed, durability, confidence, great hands, and was a very good blocker. He was a good team player. He was a guy who worked hard. He was the ideal back. He had a combination of power and speed and agility."

Gill led Nebraska in passing three straight seasons, with the 1983 season being his best, when he completed 94 of 170 passes for 1,516 yards and 14 touchdowns. And if they had given assists in college football for high option pitches, he would have been a great point guard.

"Turner was great, he knew exactly where I would be at, and he'd get me the ball at the right time at the right moment," Rozier said. "That's the thing about football, you've got to know what the other players around you can do. That's the way it was for me, Turner, and Irving. I knew Irving would block for me downfield, he loved to block field. And I knew when Turner was going to give me the ball, and I knew when he threw it, he'd throw it well."

In 1983 Fryar had 40 receptions for 780 yards (19.5 yards a catch) and eight touchdowns. He also was very dangerous as a runner after he caught the ball and on reverses. His specialty was big plays.

"It is obvious, to beat us you would have to slow down the ground game because everything we built was off of that and getting the ball to Mike," said Solich, who was in his first season as the Cornhuskers running backs coach. "He averaged nearly eight yards a carry that season. Nobody did slow him down. What came off that was play-action passes to Irving. We used his speed coming off play-action passes."

The Triplets, at least the two New Jersey players, socialized.

"We had a little house we'd always go to," Rozier said. "Nate Mason [quarterback] and Ricky Simmons [split end] had a house over by the Devaney Center. Most of the players went to our parties, and everybody hung at that house. Roger Craig, Irving, and myself, we kept it a little family thing. We kept it all in the family."

Nebraska's closest game during the 1983 regular season was a 14–10 victory over Oklahoma State in Stillwater.

"We had a shot to the end zone at the end of the game to win it," said Oklahoma State's head coach at the time, Pat Jones. "We were leading at half 10–7. That was the best offensive team I saw in college football....That was their high-water mark, offensively. They weren't as good defensively.

"Two years before then, Missouri lost to them 6–0 and hauled off and blitzed every down. We copied the blitz. We had Leslie O'Neal [end] and sophomore Mark Moore [defensive back]. Our strength was our defense. We ran a blitz and fired the corners and bluffed. A lot of stuff we copied from their Missouri game two years before then."

Two Points from Glory

Nebraska had been ranked number one the entire 1983 season. The Cornhuskers opened the season with a smashing 44–6 victory over Penn State in the Kickoff Classic in East Rutherford, New Jersey, and had run their overall winning streak to 22 straight games heading into the Orange Bowl showdown with fifth-ranked Miami.

Miami, behind quarterback Bernie Kosar, jumped on the Cornhuskers for a 17–0 first-quarter lead. He threw two touchdown passes to tight end Glenn Dennison, and Jeff Davis added a 45-yard field goal to stun the Cornhuskers.

Resilient Nebraska answered with a 14–0 second quarter. Turner Gill scored on a conventional one-yard run. But the first NU touchdown was offensive guard Dean Steinkuhler's "Fumbleroosky," which went in the books as a 19-yard fumble-recovery for a score. It was one of Tom Osborne's gadget plays that worked to perfection.

Nebraska tied the score at 17–17 early in the third quarter on Scott Livingston's 34-yard field goal. In the seesaw game, Miami, within a five-minute span, scored two rushing touchdowns to take a 31–17 lead into the fourth quarter.

Rozier got hurt shortly after the Hurricanes' second touchdown of the third quarter.

"I know it would have most definitely been different if I would have been able to stay in," Rozier said. "I'm pretty sure we would have won it. But unfortunately I had a bad ankle sprain. I was kind

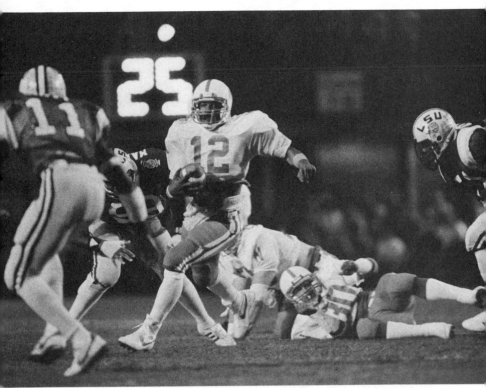

Turner Gill, the quarterback and third part of the Huskers' legendary triumvirate, came from deep in the heart of Texas.

of upset about that game. I always want to help the team out, and it hurt me that I couldn't perform because of that ankle sprain. Their defensive back cut me and sprained it. My ankle was pretty messed up for a whole year."

Nebraska's reserve I-back Jeff Smith, however, came in to rush for 99 yards and two touchdowns. He scored on a one-yard run with 6:55 remaining to slice Miami's lead to 31–24. He then scampered 24 yards for a touchdown on a fourth-and-eight play with 48 seconds remaining. Nebraska was within reach, with the score 31-30 and the extra point to come.

But no...

Osborne elected to go for two points and the victory instead of opting for a tie, which could have given Nebraska the national title, considering the Cornhuskers were actually playing on the Miami Hurricanes' home field.

"Basically, 90 percent of the fans agreed with him on the call," Nebraska fullback Scott Porter said later.

"We most definitely would have won the national championship with the tie," Rozier said. "But I'm glad we went for the win, because that year we blew everybody out. We didn't want to kick and go for the tie. We wanted the win."

When the decision was made to go for the victory, quarterback Turner Gill said he wasn't surprised.

"I knew we were going for two points," Gill said. "We were going there to win. We were going there to be 13–0. We weren't there to go to 12–0–1. I am glad he stuck with that and gave us the call and all of those things. We were just inches away from making the play. We knew the play that would be called. We had been practicing our two-point play. So I knew that would probably be the call. They made a great play.

"We tried to disguise the play, running Irving Fryar across the middle, and then we had our running back coming out in the flat. And the guy who guarded Irving didn't run with Irving. He stayed with Jeff Smith, and I made the throw to him."

Miami's strong safety, Kenny Calhoun, knocked the pass out of Smith's hands. And Miami was able to win its first national title (Associated Press) in the 50th Orange Bowl.

chapter 10
National Champs Again

Nebraska fullback Cory Schlesinger dives into the end zone for the game-winning touchdown against Miami on January 1, 1995, at the FedEx Orange Bowl in Miami.

Heading into the 1991 season, there was reason to believe the Nebraska program was slipping under Tom Osborne.

In 1990 Nebraska had dropped three of its final four games, including a whopping 45–10 defeat to Oklahoma in the last regular-season game and a 45–21 loss to Georgia Tech in the Citrus Bowl. A three-loss season, a third-place finish in the Big 8, a fourth straight bowl loss—all were not good omens.

Strength coach Boyd Epley noticed the drop-off.

"We had a series of 20 seasons where we were ranked in the top 10 [12th or higher],"Epley said in a 1996 interview. "In 1990 we dropped to 24th [in the AP poll] and 17th in the other. And we weren't sure why at first....After 20 years, we just kind of took it for granted. We had slipped, and one of the areas we had slipped in was our offensive line. We had not recruited real well across the board.

"The other area we had slipped in was the weight room, the choice of exercises, the attitude of the players, and the discipline of the players. There were maybe 10 different things we needed to do better in order to get it turned around. Coach Osborne evaluated all phases of the operation of personnel and programs. There was a rededication."

On January 17, 1991, as Nebraska prepared to start its winter program, at a team meeting of 200 players, Epley held up his national championship ring from the early 1970s under Bob Devaney. He told the players he had a plan on how to get them all one. Epley said the prevailing feeling was that talent was not a problem. In the 1991 draft Nebraska would have six draft choices, including two first-round picks—defensive back Bruce Pickens (Atlanta) and linebacker Mike Croel (Denver).

"It was attitude," Epley said. "We didn't have Nebraska's work ethic in place....We needed to get that turned around."

Soon a discipline "point system" for missing workouts (similar to driver's license points for violations) was established as was the Unity Council, a group of two players from each position, which acted as a sounding board for issues between players and coaches. There were fewer missed workouts and better relationships between coaches. Strength improved.

"We had 6,500 workouts before our first absence," Epley said. "At the time, we had been averaging 30 absences a day in 1990. One player had 130 absences in his career. The program had eroded a little bit."

There were subtle changes in defensive philosophy, from a 5–2 to a 4–3. The Cornhuskers were better able to defend the pass and rose from 49th nationally in total defense in the early 1990s, all the way to fourth in 1993 on a defense headed by first-round draft pick linebacker Trev Alberts.

The result was Nebraska won six conference titles in Osborne's final seven seasons as head coach at Nebraska and three national titles, in 1994, 1995, and 1997. The Cornhuskers won the Big 12 North Division title in 1996, the other season they failed to win the outright Big 12 title.

Quarterback Tommie Frazier: The Magic Man

A catalyst recruit was quarterback Tommie Frazier from Bradenton, Florida. He was the key to the ignition switch as the Cornhuskers geared up for their mid-1990s run.

"I called him 'Magic Man,'" former Nebraska safety Mike Minter (1993 to 1996) said. "He created plays out of nothing all the time. He would do things on the football field I haven't seen since. He meant everything to us as far as the offensive game plan was concerned."

"Frazier was one of those guys, if you needed a third-and-three, you just knew Tommie was going to do it," said guard-center Aaron Taylor, Nebraska's Outland Trophy winner in 1997. "He took command of the huddle. He would call the play. You almost had a feeling if he didn't think the play called was going to happen, he would keep the ball himself and get the first down. It was just a weird deal. You just knew he was going to do whatever it took to get it done. To me it was the third-and-threes and third-and-fours. His field vision and athletic ability were so damn good that he ended up making the play to get the first down, or whatever it was.

You kind of went back to the huddle, and thought, 'Damn, that guy is good.'

"There would be numerous option plays that you are pulling around, and you would go to kick out a defensive end, or whatever, and you see Tommie darting up and making two quick cuts, and the next thing you know it would be a first down. It might only be a six- or seven-yard run, but it was pretty amazing."

In 1992 Frazier became Nebraska's first starting freshman quarterback since World War II. He accounted for 1,126 yards of total offense, 17 touchdowns, and 125.1 yards of offense a game as Nebraska went 9–3 and lost to Florida State 27–14 in the Orange Bowl.

A year later Frazier and Nebraska had a close brush with a national championship when the Cornhuskers won their first 11 games and a third straight Big 8 title. Frazier's numbers were even better, when he accounted for 1,863 yards of total offense (1,159 passing, 704 rushing) and 21 total touchdowns.

Number-two Nebraska took an 11–0 record into the 1994 Orange Bowl and was a 17-point underdog to top-ranked Florida State, but had a chance to win on the final play of the game when Byron Bennett's 45-yard field-goal attempt was wide left. Scott Bentley's 22-yard field goal with 21 seconds remaining had made Florida State an 18–16 winner.

"It was then when I think we began to grow up as a unit, as a university, and as a team," Minter said of that game. "There was 1:16 on the clock when they got the ball. Every time we went out and practiced, we had that 1:16 up there on the clock, so we could remember how long it took for us to lose that football game. So I think it motivated us in a whole other way. That prepared us to do what we did in the next couple of years."

The 1994 season did not turn out personally for Frazier like the previous two. Because of blood clots in his right knee, Frazier was forced out after the fourth game and would finish with just 521 yards of total offense. Osborne played Brook Berringer, who suffered a partially collapsed lung, but compiled a 7–0 record as a starter. For one game, Osborne finally was down to walk-on

Freshman quarterback phenom Tommie Frazier runs for a touchdown in the second quarter of the Coca-Cola Bowl at the Tokyo Dome in Japan in December 5, 1992. Frazier ran for three touchdowns and helped Nebraska beat Kansas State 38–24.

quarterback Matt Turman, who got the nickname "the Turmanator." He beat Kansas State 17–6 on the way to a meeting against Miami on the Hurricanes' home field in the Orange Bowl. Another national title was at stake.

By this time, both Frazier and Berringer were healthy. And Osborne elected to start Frazier in this high-stakes game, then alternate them. Berringer was the quarterback whom Osborne planned to ride to the end. But with Nebraska trailing 17–9 and the national title on the line, Osborne went back to Frazier, who directed Nebraska to two fourth-quarter scores with the option game.

"You get behind, playing catch-up with an option football team is tough," Fiala said. "But for Tommie to come in and win that game—Tommie started the game. Brook came in, and Tommie came back in and had a fresh set of legs on him. And the Miami people were pretty exhausted. And Tommie just ran over them and won that game."

The Nebraska Fullback Legends

While Frazier won the MVP award for the Orange Bowl game, he completed just three of five passes for 25 yards and ran for only 31 yards. Yet his ability to create an option that Miami had to stop on the ground opened up the fullback series for Nebraska and allowed Cory Schlesinger to score touchdowns of 15 and 14 yards to win the game.

"I think what typified what Nebraska was all about is what you saw in that championship game—being physical, pounding you, and winning the game in the second half, in the fourth quarter," Minter said. "And that's what we did with a very talented defense in Miami. We just started popping them straight up the middle. Our fullback had a big day."

Epley said the Miami game showed how the Nebraska strength program had improved in four years.

"It is probably the most dramatic illustration of physical superiority that I have ever seen in a football game, pro or college," Epley said. "Miami got so tired in the fourth quarter that we physically dominated them."

Nebraska assistant coach at the time, Frank Solich, explained that the fullback philosophy at Nebraska was a science.

"We were running a ball-controlled offense under Tom," Solich said. "And really that was similar to Devaney's thinking. And they used the fullback in quick-hitting plays. Cory Schlesinger was the fullback in that game. And typically you look at fullbacks in systems now, and if they get one or two carries a game, that is a big surprise. They are used only as blockers. But in Tom's system things were built off the option game, so the fullback would have enough carries and come off that with options.

"Look at the great fullbacks in his system. Schlesinger and before that, Tom Rathman, Andra Franklin, and then Jeff Makovicka. It was a position guys liked to play because not only did they play a very physical position in terms of blocking, they also got their chance to get their hands on the ball some and could show what they were about athletically."

The victory also gave Osborne his first national title.

"It meant everything [to get Osborne his first national title] because it was so hard," Minter said. "They were being hard on him because they always said he couldn't win the big one. So when he started to win the big one, it was everything. But like I told you, since third grade, when he lost the championship to Miami, I was watching that game. And I wanted to go [to Nebraska]. So for me, watching that game as a young kid and then years later to be able to deliver a championship to Coach Osborne, that was something."

The 1995 Season: Peters' Pregame Defensive Antics

The Cornhuskers entered the 1995 season as the defending national champions and ranked second. Starting with a 64–21 Thursday night victory at Oklahoma State on ESPN, the Cornhuskers won 12 straight games. They moved up to number one in early November and stayed there.

With Frazier back at the controls and the Cornhuskers deep at I-back, the offense produced more than 70 points twice and more than 60 points in two other games. The smallest scoring output was a 35–21 victory over Washington State. The defense was outstanding as well.

On that 1995 active roster were numerous defensive stand-outs who later played in the NFL. Among them were tackles Jason and Christian Peter, ends Jared Tomich and Grant Wistrom, line-backers Doug Colman and Jamel Williams, safety Mike Minter, cornerbacks Tyrone Williams and Michael Booker, and free safety Tony Veland.

"You knew [in a game] you weren't going to face anyone as good as Jason or Christian Peter or a Wistrom or a Tomich," Taylor said. "Going against those guys in practice, you knew you were going to have a break on Saturday. None of the guys [on the opponent's defensive line] were going to be as good as the guys you were practicing against.

"They [the Peters] were probably the hardest working guys. Jason was working on his run stopping, he could stop the pass; Christian could stop the run; but he was always working on his pass-rushing skills. You just knew every time you lined up against those guys you were going to have a versatile defensive linemen that could do multiple things and you were never going to get less than 100 percent. Never."

And the Peter brothers were the craziest of them all.

"Those guys would be so fired up before a game, they were jumping around, knocking chalkboards down, kicking lockers in," Minter recalled. "When you look at a movie and you see the crazy players you see in a movie, that's the type of players we had. They would hit their heads against the locker, just going crazy, getting everybody pumped up and excited. And don't let anybody talk trash about us before the game, because we really be going crazy if that was the situation."

Taylor remembers the Peter boys giving a pregame pep talk before Nebraska played Michigan State in East Lansing for the second game of the 1995 season.

"The Peter brothers had family from Michigan, so growing up, they would send a lot of Michigan State gear to the Peter brothers for Christmas," Taylor said. "Christian, who sported a bald head, was giving the pregame speech. And he must have had his parents send him a Michigan State wall clock that Jason holds up. And Christian shoves his fist through this wall clock.

"'When we grew up we were taught to love Michigan State, and we can't stand those bastards, blah-blah-blah,' they said. And they end up beating the clock down and just torturing the clock. Then Christian grabs a Christmas ornament ball. It was green with a Michigan State helmet and logo on it. And, as he is talking, he crashes it over his head. You know what those are made out of? Glass. And he starts bleeding profusely."

Because this was a players-only meeting for the pregame speech, the trainers weren't there. So Christian Peter, the adrenaline flowing, talked for about three or four more minutes, not realizing the extent of his self-inflicted wound.

"And everybody's eyes get as big as saucers, holy cow!" Taylor continued. "He has that bald head and he is bleeding and he goes on for another few minutes. Finally, when we go into our team prayer, somebody hands him a towel. I think he ended up starting the game. But he had to get bandaged up. It was probably one of the craziest things I had ever seen in my life."

Nebraska wound up winning the Michigan State game 50–10. That evening a development with standout I-back Lawrence Phillips would make national headlines and basically end his bright future at Nebraska.

Lawrence Phillips: A Wasted Talent

I-back Lawrence Phillips, from West Covina, California, had a troubled background and had been suspended before by Osborne for a couple of lesser offenses. But he led Nebraska in rushing in 1994 with 1,722 yards rushing on 286 carries and had the third-best per-game rushing average in college football during the 1994 season. His rushing average was 6.0 yards a carry, and he scored 16 touchdowns for the defending national champions.

Then, after the 1995 Michigan State game, Phillips was arrested and later convicted of assaulting former girlfriend Kate McEwen. Phillips went to the apartment of teammate quarterback Scott Frost, found McEwen there, grabbed her by the hair, and dragged her down three flight of stairs. He then held her by the throat until Frost and another man rescued her.

Initially Osborne believed Phillips's career as a Nebraska football player was over. He ended up providing McEwen with 24-hour security. But Taylor said Osborne went to the Nebraska players' Unity Council to make the decision if Phillips should be kicked entirely out of the program.

"He let us make the decision whether to keep Lawrence or kick him off the team," Taylor said. "He made a couple of stipulations. He said, 'If you guys decide to keep him on the team, this is what he has to do for me to stay on the team.' He had to show up for counseling sessions and other certain things at certain times. Coach Osborne said, 'If he misses one of them, he is not coming back. You let me know what you guys decide.'"

Taylor said the Unity Council talked for about 35 to 45 minutes about Phillips.

"And never once did we feel like we needed Lawrence to win the national title," Taylor said. "We had Damon Benning. We had Ahman Green. We also had a guy, Clinton Childs. What we finally decided is Lawrence never really had had a family. He never had a history of someone sticking with him and helping him through a problem in his life.

"He was brought up in group homes throughout his whole life. He never really truly had a family. And once he got out of that family atmosphere, which was his football team, that's where it all kind of fell apart for him.

"We came down with the decision: we recommended that he stay on the football team, that he gets support or the help that he needs in order to get through this. And then if he does make it all the way though, that means he may be on the team but never may see the field, dress up, or walk into the locker room. He ended up playing in the bowl game [against Florida]."

Because Phillips had met Osborne's and the Unity Council's requirements for reinstatement, including receiving counseling, he was allowed to play in the Fiesta Bowl.

"From my point of view, he was probably one of the best teammates I had. In the locker room, he wasn't an instigator. He wasn't a hell raiser. He wasn't a bad teammate. In practice, you would never see a guy who would run out a player any harder or who would work as hard as he did. I don't recall him ever missing a practice. Even during the games, you never heard him bitching or moaning about not getting the ball, or his linemen missing a block, or his fullback missing a block, or the quarterback keeping the ball on a pitch on the option. And you saw what an unbelievable athlete he was with speed, power, vision, and quickness."

Despite his troubles at Nebraska, Phillips was selected in the first round of the 1996 NFL Draft by the St. Louis Rams, had more trouble with the law, played two seasons in St. Louis, and then bounced around to a bunch of teams in the NFL, NFL Europe, and the Canadian Football League.

With Phillips basically out of the picture early in the 1995 season, Green, an Omaha native and true freshman, became Nebraska's leading rusher that season. In fact, he was the Cornhuskers' leading rusher for the next three seasons. Green would top off his career at Nebraska with 1,877 yards rushing as a junior in 1997.

"You knew right away he was going to be special," said Kris Brown, a freshman kicker on that 1995 Nebraska team. "He had this combination of speed and power. He could run between the tackles. That '95 year he was probably the third running back on our team."

But Green was ready to go when Phillips was sent to counseling.

"I wanted to do whatever my team needed me to do," Green said. "I didn't want to redshirt. I knew I could play. I learned that in camp, that I could play college football. I'll do anything on the field not to redshirt. I got a lot of backup time before I started, played on special teams like kickoff returns. I was always a hard worker and still am. I learned by watching the older guys in practice and busting my butt. I got a lot of time early in my career."

Green said Phillips even helped him through his first season.

"He was a big help," Green said. "He kept me motivated. Even when he was suspended, he was always in the weight room. He was still taking classes. He talked to me and let me know I was doing a good job and what I needed to do to get better."

Winning Another Title in 1995

Green was more than adequate replacement. And there was no match for Nebraska on its 1995 schedule. The Cornhuskers breezed through the Big 8 in its final season with a 7–0 record before the Big 12 began operation in 1996. In fact, Nebraska won its final 23 games of Big 8 competition, dating to a November 14, 1992, loss at Iowa State.

Ahman Green (30) gets away from Oklahoma defensive back Wendell Davis (28) during the first quarter in Lincoln, Nebraska, Friday, November 24, 1995.

"We kept winning games," Green said. "When I got in the game, I did my job. I made my first start versus Missouri, a 57–0 win. I had, like, 96 yards rushing and a couple touchdowns. Before that I was getting my 100 yards a pop as a backup."

A 37–0 victory over archrival Oklahoma in the last Big 8 Conference game in 1995 wrapped up the Osborne era in that league. The only thing left to do was play number-two Florida in the Fiesta Bowl for the national championship.

"Now you look back and think about that team," said Brown. "I saw a stat that for the entire season—we only trailed for 13 minutes. Our smallest margin of victory was 35–21. You look back on it now you appreciate it a lot more. The way college football is now, it's not like that. I don't know if it will ever be like that again. The parity has gotten a lot tighter. It gives you an appreciation for '95 and the whole four years."

Brown anticipated that the game between the number-one and -two teams in the country would be close.

"Florida pretty much dominated every game," Brown said. "We dominated every game we played. Conventional wisdom was that

Tom Osborne gets doused in the closing minutes by quarterback Tommie Frazier and teammates after the 62–24 drubbing of Florida in the 1996 Fiesta Bowl to give Nebraska the national championship.

special teams would be an important part of the game. It could come down to a kick. I took it like any other game. I think I missed my first extra point. It got it blocked. The second quarter it ended up being a rout. At the time I didn't realize it."

But Nebraska overwhelmed Florida 62–24 in the Fiesta Bowl. Trailing 10–6 after one quarter, Nebraska blew out the Gators with a 29-point second quarter. In the game, Florida quarterback Danny Wuerffel was intercepted three times and was thrown for 37 yards in losses by the Blackshirts.

"People didn't realize we were just as fast as they were," Minter said. "So you have two things that cancel each other out. So what else do you bring to the table? We were physical, too.

We were going to slow them down by hitting them hard and getting to their quarterback. We knew if we gave him time to throw the football, he might cause some problems for us. The thing I told my guys was to go in there and be physical. We know we can run with them. So when we get there, we have to punch them."

Frazier in his final game was brilliant with 199 yards rushing (12.4-yards-per-carry average), and he added 105 yards passing. In his return and final game as a Cornhusker, Phillips carried the ball 25 times for 165 yards and two touchdowns. He also added a touchdown with a pass reception from Frazier, whose touchdown runs covered 75 and 35 yards.

It Happened That Spring

In the spring of 1996, a terrible tragedy befell the Nebraska football program when former NU quarterback Brook Berringer died in a plane crash on April 18. Berringer had graduated from Nebraska the previous December and was expected to be selected in the NFL Draft a few days later.

After serving as Tommie Frazier's backup during the 1994 season, he became the starter after Frazier developed blood clots in his right knee in the fourth game. Berringer was 7–0 as a starter in Nebraska's 1995 national title year and was considered a professional prospect despite his mostly back-up status at Nebraska.

"I was in class in the East Campus and I had heard one of my classmates say they had heard Brook was in a plane crash," Taylor said. "I knew he flew planes all the time. I turned 'round and went back to my car to see if I could hear it on the radio. And I remember I literally sat in my car for an hour and a half just listening to the details of what had happened with the plane crash. They had people calling in. I ended up skipping class because I was in my car in utter shock. And there were people calling in with their memories of Brook already.

"Brook was a guy who had friends all over the locker room. Not just his little clique or his group. He was a guy who was friends with everyone. He was an All-America guy. He is someone I would want my daughter to marry. Caring, generous, all of those. He was two years older than me. There was no reason for us to hang out or go hunting or any of that, and we would do that every now and then. He invited me to fly back to Goodland, Kansas, with him and take his hunting dogs back. Of course, I didn't do that. I didn't do that because he asked me how much I weighed and that could determine how much fuel he could put on the plane."

"The whole team felt that," I-back Ahman Green said. "The whole state felt that when he passed."

Desert Outfoxed in 1996

Nebraska entered the second game of the 1996 season at Arizona State with impressive credentials and gunning for a third straight national title. Nebraska had the longest wining streak in college football—26 straight games. The Cornhuskers had won 37 straight regular-season games and had held the top spot in the rankings 12 straight weeks.

What happened at Sun Devil Stadium was one of the most shocking upsets of nearly any season. The Sun Devils shut out Nebraska's powerhouse offense 19–0. In the final tally, it was one of only three times (twice in the regular season) that a Tom Osborne–coached team was shut out at Nebraska in his 25-year head-coaching tenure there, from 1973 to 1997. The other times were 27–0 by Oklahoma in Osborne's first season as head coach in 1973 and 22–0 to Miami in the 1992 Orange Bowl.

"The Arizona State game probably was the weirdest experience I had in my life," said Nebraska's Outland Trophy–winner Aaron Taylor. "This was another case of wanting to practice the night before the game. But there were probably 2,000 people on the field having dinner the night before the game because they were renaming the field Frank Kush Field [after the former Arizona State coach]. And people were drunk at that thing. We were dressed, ready to go to practice. They were bad-mouthing us and bad-mouthing the coaches.

"The next day was probably the longest day," Taylor continued. "It was a night game. It was a weird, long day. It was the loudest game that I have been to in my life. Ever been to a concert and stood beside one of those big, old, stand-up speakers and you feel your body vibrating? That is the way it was down on the field. And I was the center that year. That was my junior year. Scott Frost, our quarterback, would be going through his cadence, 2–22, 2–22, and I couldn't hear him. He was right behind me. We would call a play in the huddle and then maybe audible 60 percent of the time. You couldn't hear the audible, line call, the cadence. It was that way from the moment we took the field until the moment we left."

The 17ᵗʰ-ranked Sun Devils took a 7–0 lead on the same field where Nebraska had pulverized Florida in the Fiesta Bowl the previous season. Nebraska had also trailed the Gators early in that game, before winning 62–24. So there was no need for panic. But this would be a completely different game.

"The story of the game was they just whipped us," Osborne said to reporters after the game, also noting that Nebraska did not generate a solid enough running game to take the heat off the passing game.

Taylor's memory served him correctly on cadence, line calls, audibles, etc. On Nebraska's first three plays, the Cornhuskers were called for a false start and a hold. Later, he snapped the ball over Frost's head, and it wound up in the end zone for a safety.

"We knew a lot about their offense," said Arizona State coach Bruce Snyder, whose team had dropped an embarrassing 77–28 decision to the Cornhuskers the previous season in Lincoln. "But the one thing we didn't know about was Scott Frost. Maybe he was the next Tommie Frazier. We didn't know. But we decided that we wanted to take everything else away and see if Scott Frost can beat us."

Frost, a Nebraska native who had gone to Stanford but transferred back to Nebraska, certainly couldn't in this game. Facing a second-and-24 at his own 6-yard line and trailing 7–0, Frost pitched the ball to Green, who fumbled the ball out of the end zone. Arizona State recorded the first of three safeties in the game, a record against a Nebraska team. Frost could never get on track against a fired-up ASU defense, which limited him to 6-for-20 and 66 yards passing, and sacked him three times.

Arizona State end Derrick Rodgers had 10 tackles (three unassisted) and a sack of Frost for one of the safeties. Sun Devils free safety Mitchell Freedman forced three fumbles, recovered one, and added three tackles.

"What happens, we couldn't block Rodgers," said former Nebraska safety Mike Minter. "He was killing us. We tried to block him all game. Those guys were fired up. At the same time, they weren't a bad football team. They went all the way and had a chance to go to the Rose Bowl and play for the national championship. So they were no slouches. That was a crazy night. They played great defense that night."

Nebraska was limited to 226 yards of offense and suffered a serious dent to its national title hopes.

"It also was one of those games where you felt like you were doing things the right way, but you were never getting the break," Taylor said. "Ahman Green would break a 30-yard run and then get tripped up by his shoe lace. He would break a 40-yard run and fumble at the end—just stuff that would never happen to you before."

After the victory that made Arizona State 3-0 for the first time since 1982, Arizona State defensive tackle Shawn Swayda said, "Last year we went into their stadium, and they embarrassed us real bad. Nobody gave us a chance to win this game. I think even the coaches had their doubts. On Friday night, we said, 'Hey, everyone is doubting us. We're the only ones who think we can win this thing.' And we did."

Rolling to a Big 12 Championship Game

After the loss to Arizona State, Nebraska dropped to eighth in the ratings, its lowest spot in the Associated Press poll since early in the 1993 season. But Scott Frost started to develop as a quarterback,

Ahman Green was an I-back star, and Nebraska had a killer defense that would show itself in this inaugural season of the new Big 12 Conference.

The league may have changed from the old Big 8, but the addition of Texas, Texas A&M, Baylor, and Texas Tech had done nothing to alter the air of invincibility of Nebraska football thus far. Nebraska rolled to an 8–0 league record, beating fifth-ranked Colorado 17–12, in the final game of the regular season for the Big 12 North Division title.

"You play with a lot of athletes, but Frost, whether it was basketball, he was a heck of a golfer, he could run, throw the shot put, hurdles, high jump," Taylor said. "He was one of the best pure athletes I have ever played with. But he was replacing Tommie Frazier. He had gone to Stanford. Then he transferred back to the state. There was almost a lot of, 'Ha, ha, you are back!' The 1996 season was tough, coming off two back-to-back titles, breaking in a new quarterback, a new fullback, and a new I-back. You are also bringing in two new people on the offensive line, plus me switching positions. Scott, his junior year, was still new to the whole option offense. He really didn't win over the Nebraska fans and leave his legacy at Nebraska until the Washington game his senior year."

But even as a junior, Frost set the table: a meeting with unranked Texas in the first Big 12 title game at the Trans World Dome in St. Louis. The indoor home of the St. Louis Rams provided the perfect warm haven for the legions of Nebraska football fans who would snap up tickets to the event and greatly outnumber their counterparts from Texas.

Despite the obvious edge in fan support Nebraska would have in St. Louis, Osborne was wary of such games. In the formation of the Big 12 Conference, Osborne and several other coaches had argued against a title game between the division winners because of this exact reason. Nebraska, despite the early loss, had worked its way back up to third in the Associated Press rankings. Without the title game, the Cornhuskers would have a better shot at the national title because they would not have to risk their ranking in an extra game.

Texas was 7–4 overall and 20½-point underdogs to the once-beaten Cornhuskers.

Ricky Williams would win the Heisman Trophy two years later. But in the title game, Texas used him as a blocker against Nebraska's standout ends Grant Wistrom and Jared Tomich. And UT's Priest Holmes gained 120 rushing yards and scored three touchdowns.

"Williams made about 20 big blocks in that game," said former UT running backs coach Bucky Godbolt. "I think it was the best game he ever played. He blocked All-Americas on every play. He picked one up and body-slammed them. He blocked the entire game one-on-one, and he enjoyed this game."

"Texas was pretty damn good," Taylor said. "Texas always has good athletes. Whether or not they put it altogether and would win ballgames is a question. It was a hard-fought game. We were having some difficulty on offense, but we were still moving the ball and scoring touchdowns. But we could never stop them."

The game came down to a fourth-and-inches play with Texas leading 30–27, with 2:48 remaining in the game at its own 28. The prevailing thought on the sideline was that Texas, under Coach John Mackovic, needed to keep the ball away from Nebraska's high-octane offense or the Cornhuskers would win the game.

"I was prepared to punt," Mackovic said. "But when they stretched the chain and we needed two inches, I thought, heck, if you are going to be a champion, you have to go for it. You have to seize the day."

Nebraska's defense was expecting a sneak by UT quarterback James Brown. Brown was to run if he saw a hole, but he also was to fake a handoff to Holmes and throw if there was no hole. If the defense bit, as it often does on the fake to Holmes, there would be a receiver wide open.

Brown, hounded by roverback Minter, lifted a pass to Derek Lewis, a sophomore tight end, who caught the ball at the UT 43 and rambled down to the Cornhusker 11 before he was caught. Texas scored on the next play, won the Big 12 title, and advanced to the Fiesta Bowl. Nebraska saw its hopes of a third-straight national title die. The Cornhuskers dropped to sixth in the AP rankings and went to the Orange Bowl, where they beat 10th-ranked Virginia Tech 41–21.

"Minter was a hell of player, even a better guy," Taylor said. "Minter was in a tough position because we had a guy, Terrell Farley, who was suspended. He actually was kicked off the team at that time. He was our linebacker. Minter was moved up from the strong safety spot to play linebacker. Basically he was 20 pounds under weight. He still had a hell of a game."

Minter said he has replayed that play a million times in his head over the last decade or so. "They came in with two tight ends and three backs in the backfield and then add the quarterback," he said. "So you think they are going to run the ball up the middle. What happened is, when we looked at the film later on, we had a cornerback Ralph Brown, who was a freshman and a very good football player. He was in the 'A' gap. He had the tight end who was wide open and caught the ball. He was supposed to cover the tight end, but he was in the 'A' gap trying to stop the quarterback sneak or the play up the middle because that is what we thought they were going to do.

"When James Brown rolled out, I was actually coming to get him," Minter recalled. "And when you watch the film, you see me coming right at him. And when he threw the ball, I was in his face. And I jumped up because I knew that play was going to come down to me knocking him backwards. I thought he was going to run. And when he threw it, I jumped and I asked myself, 'Who is he throwing it to?' And I looked back and there was a man wide open."

An Odd Trail to the Outland Trophy

Aaron Taylor really wasn't recruited much out of Wichita Falls, Texas. The son of an Air Force father, he had lived overseas and played soccer. He didn't have much size. He was a Texas A&M fan growing up because family friends lived in College Station.

In 1997 he became the seventh different Cornhusker to win the Outland Trophy, which is awarded to the best interior lineman in college football. He edged out 1997 teammate defensive tackle Jason Peter and joined Larry Jacobson (1971), Rich Glover (1972), Dave Rimington (1981–1982), Dean Steinkuhler (1983), Will Shields (1992), and Zach Wiegert (1994)—all former Nebraska winners.

"A&M said I was too short," Taylor explained. "I really didn't get recruited much by Texas. And Texas Tech, I actually took a visit to Texas Tech. I came back and then I never got another phone call from them.

"My high school coach asked me about it. I told him I hadn't heard anything from Texas Tech for a while. And he calls up Spike Dykes [Texas Tech's coach then], and they said Spike Dykes felt I was too short to play, and they offered a kid out of California. They told me if he didn't take it, I could have the scholarship. So that kind of ticked me off. I never got an offer from them. I told my coach to contact TCU. So he called TCU. And they mentioned they had seen my game film, but they didn't think I was good enough to play Division I football. So he got pissed and said he knew why their program was where it was at and hung up the phone."

Nebraska had recruited Taylor the entire time. Nebraska's line coach Milt Tenopir asked Taylor who had recruited him.

"I wanted to lie and tell him everybody in the world," Taylor recalled. "And I couldn't. I said they are all concerned about my height. He said to me in his terms, 'I don't care how high you are. I care about the size of your heart.' And he went on to mention he had had Will Shields, who was a Outland Trophy winner who wasn't much over 6'1". And he had a 12- or 13-year career (14) in the NFL."

Taylor's first season was the national title season of 1994. And in 1995 he started at left guard before he was asked to make a position switch his junior season to center.

"We just never had anybody who was developing at center," Taylor said. "So after we won the national title that year, in 1995, it was like, 'Who is going to take over the center spot?' And Milt Tenopir asked if I would like to take that over. He came to me and said, 'Hey, we don't have anyone developed ready to step in and play center. We feel you are our most versatile athlete, would you mind doing that?' You don't tell Coach Tenopir no.

"It was an interesting transition. I never played center in my life. I didn't mind playing center. But in the Nebraska scheme, when you were a guard, you got out and pulled or trap blocked. You were just more involved in the offense. When you played center, you made some line calls, but to me you never got your nose into things. You never had the ability to go out and get nasty. That is why I wanted to move back to guard so bad. And then my senior year we finally had a guy who had developed center named Josh Heskew."

But Taylor made All-America as a center in 1996, so he was ready for a big year in 1997, as were the Cornhuskers.

In the 1997 season, Taylor's senior year when the Cornhuskers won their third national title in four years, he had moved back to guard and was the only offensive starter out of 11 players who did not hail from the state of Nebraska. It was a bit unusual to have all the skilled players' spots filled by Nebraskans. The backfield was Scott Frost (Wood River), Ahman Green (Omaha), and Joel Makovicka (Brainard). The starting tight end was Tim Carpenter from Columbus. Both receivers, Lance Brown (Papillion) and Jeff Lake (Columbus), grew up in the state as well.

That Special 1997 Season

In 1997 Nebraska beat 13 straight teams. The closest game was the 45–38 overtime victory over Missouri. From the 1997 team, Wistrom and Peter were both first-round draft choices. Green went in the third round, as did Frost; Taylor not until the seventh round.

"It was special because it was my last year in college," Green said. "It was kind of my team. I was one of the leaders. Scott Frost,

Jason Peter, Aaron Taylor, Grant Wistrom—they were seniors. I was the junior leader [but that was his last season before turning professional]. It was kind of like we did it with a new group of guys."

Green, years later with the Houston Texans of the NFL, looked back on that era with fondness.

"I came in there and did my job to the best of my ability, and did well," Green said. "I think I'm second in career rushing behind Mike Rozier. I didn't get a chance to win the Heisman, but I helped my team to two national titles. I'll take that any day. I'm not complaining at all. I loved it."

Actually, when Green got to Nebraska he requested No. 34, his high school number. A junior tight end already had it and wouldn't give it up. The coaches suggested he wear No. 30, the uniform that Mike Rozier carried to the Heisman Trophy. "You really want me to wear this?" asked Green. "I didn't expect to do what he had done. I expected to do what I can do. I never felt the pressure from wearing 30. Once I got it, I got used to having it."

Green rushed for 1,877 yards as a senior and finished second behind Rozier on the Cornhuskers' career rushing charts. Frost had 2,332 yards of total offense that season, one yard shy of the Nebraska season record at the time held by quarterback Jerry Tagge.

In 1997 Nebraska won a split national title when it beat Tennessee 42–17 in the Orange Bowl in Osborne's final game. Michigan was number one in the Associated Press poll. Nebraska was first in the USA Today Coaches' poll.

Osborne went out in style. The Cornhuskers piled up 534 yards of total offense against number-three Tennessee. They ended the game with a touchdown drive of nine straight running plays and staked their claim to the national title.

"If you ask me, I don't think it should be a split national title," Jason Peter said after the game. "I mean, we proved today that we're the best in the country."

Compared to the tumultuous 1995 national title season when the Phillips' ordeal and other disciplinary issues surfaced, 1997 was a snap for Osborne, who credited the decision by Wistrom, the 1997 Lombardi Trophy winner, and Peter to return for their senior years as big reasons the team won the national title. Osborne said he didn't have to do much.

Of course, a member of his staff, Turner Gill, who was also the quarterback at Nebraska, said Osborne did an awful lot. Gill listed these as the highpoints of his career.

"Becoming a Division I football player, and becoming a starting quarterback [against Colorado], and winning a national championship as a coach, three national titles, and being undefeated for two and a half years," Gill said, "Coach Osborne started and reached his goal—seeing a great coach doing things the right way and treating people the right way and showing people you can be a nice guy and still win."

chapter 11

Walk-ons, Weight Lifting, Redshirting, Fan Adoration: The Culture of Nebraska

The Huskers, shown here practicing for the January 1, 1994, Orange Bowl game against Florida State University, have always been known for their blue-collar work ethic.

The beginnings of a weight program at Nebraska in the late 1960s folded into a football culture where walk-ons, redshirting, and big, powerful offensive lines went hand-in-hand and created a powerhouse football program that lasted 30 years.

Strength czar Boyd Epley eventually created the Taj Mahal of weight training and conditioning facilities at Nebraska, a far cry for the original beginnings—a small, dark room with a Universal gym and a few free weights.

Epley's weight-lifting program helped create the foundation for Tom Osborne's program. Starting in 1973, his first season, and running through 1997, Osborne's teams never lost more than three games in a season, won three national titles, claimed 13 conference titles, and went to 25 straight bowls.

Recruiting, molding, and solidifying the offensive line became a science in Epley's weight-lifting and conditioning incubator. While rumors and even some admissions of steroid and perform-ance-enhancing drug use have swirled around some former Nebraska players, the success of Osborne's offensive system never wavered.

In an interview a decade ago, Epley firmly said Osborne would not tolerate steroid use.

"He is a coach who believed in running the ball, and in order to run the ball, you have to have an offensive line that can move the defense out of the way," Epley said in a 1996 interview. "So you recruit for a certain type of kid who can do that. In recruiting, you know you have this strength program. You recruit kids who are willing to work hard and have the potential to grow into what you want. You don't recruit kids who are short and squatty. You recruited kids who had a certain body type, so when they do plug into the strength program, four or five years later, they will have a certain look to them. Then, you are going to have the offensive line to run the ball."

Redshirting was part of the process. And with the numbers Nebraska had with its walk-on program, it had the luxury to build players through this process.

"It takes years to get strong," Epley said. "And so to give a kid some extra time, you redshirt him. You give him another year to perform. They get redshirted their freshmen or sophomore years, and they have three years to develop."

"Redshirting gives players the opportunity to mature physically and mentally," said former Nebraska quarterback and NU assistant Turner Gill, now the head coach of the University at Buffalo. "You are never 100 percent perfect in recruiting. You would miss on some scholarship players. By redshirting players, by their junior or senior years, particularly walk-ons would be ready to play and they would be just like [good] scholarship players. This would be particularly true of positions like tight ends, fullbacks, and the offensive line, where there were a lot of walk-ons. It helped Nebraska to never have a bad year.

"By keeping players in the program five years, the players also had a better understanding of the system and the assistant coaches. That bred continuity and, in the final analysis, winning."

Jim Dickey, the head coach at Kansas State from 1978 to 1985, saw this process up close. And he redshirted several players going into their senior seasons of 1981. The next season, with those fifth-year seniors at the core, Kansas State finished the regular season 6–4–1 and went to its first bowl game in history.

"We were always playing 20-year-old kids against 22-year-old kids at Nebraska," Dickey said. "It just happened. Those guys said something about doing it. I thought two weeks before the season they would back out. Once it got started, it stayed like that. It definitely helped us. We were bigger and more physical and we had a hell of a year. Even in the losses we had, we looked like we belonged on the field. It was a deal of the kids being bulked up and strong....I am certainly not an authority. If you can get a pretty good offensive line, you can stick anybody back there and it makes it look good."

Nebraska had annually one of the best offensive lines in the country, including five Outland Trophy winners on the offensive line from 1981 to 1997: center Dave Rimington (1981 and 1982); guard Dean Steinkuhler (1983), guard Will Shields (1992), tackle Zach Wiegert (1994), and guard Aaron Taylor (1997).

Wiegert and two other future NFL offensive linemen, guard Brenden Stai and tackle Rob Zatechka, were redshirted their first years on campus and had to practice on the scout team against the varsity, instead of playing on the freshman team. All were selected in the first four rounds of the 1995 draft and played in the NFL.

How strong was Stai when he was a fifth-year senior? Taylor showed up as a wide-eyed freshman in the 1994 preseason camp, ran into him, and found out.

"It was the second or third day after the veterans reported," he said. "And I had to play defense during individual drills. I remembered I stepped up to the line of scrimmage. And I saw Brenden Stai coming down the line pulling. And I didn't think I was a bad athlete. He literally picks me up and the first thing to hit the ground was the back of my head. That is when I questioned myself, 'Do I really belong here?' I had never had anything like that happen to me ever before. I was scared. He was 6'5", 320 pounds. I never said anything to him. It was the biggest eye-opener I ever had. I can still remember it. I can walk you right to the place right now on the field."

The tutelage of Nebraska's offensive linemen during that era came from Milt Tenopir, a Nebraska assistant coach from 1974 to 2002 and the first non-Outland winner to have a trophy. He manufactured linemen like Detroit does cars after learning from one of the great Nebraska linemen in the late 1940s, Cletus Fischer, a Nebraska assistant from 1959 to 1985.

"It gets way back in the days of Cletus Fischer and later as offensive line coach," said Adrian Fiala. "It is just the way he coached players and the kind of confidence he instilled in people. We got into the strength and conditioning program, and the big guys up front seemed to excel in that. Cletus Fischer had a lot of ability as a coach. Milt Tenopir, he was an assistant under Clete and learned under Clete."

From 1975 to 1997, Osborne won 13 league titles. And along with its nemesis Oklahoma, Nebraska had a grinding offense that dominated the Big 8.

"I think they had a great grasp of exactly what they wanted to do," said Pat Jones, who was at Oklahoma State 11 years as head coach, from 1984 to 1994, and five as an assistant, from 1979 to 1983. "At times they were pretty predictable, but they were so solid, fundamentally sound. They were pretty adaptable and gifted. At times you knew what happened and couldn't do anything about it. Then you thought you had an answer, and they would counter with something."

"They put good linemen out there," added Dickey, who lost every game to Nebraska during his Kansas State tenure. "Sure they had good I-backs. But they would have two or three kids a year on the offensive line get drafted. It was a joke saying, 'It's what's up front that counts!' Everybody started with Nebraska with respect for the offensive linemen. You would trot out there and watch them warm up. And you would want to play good. But the thing was over because they were too big."

"They had big, strong linemen," said former Kansas State tight end Eddy Whitley (1976 to 1979). "Their weight program and their conditioning program was ahead of the majority of folks. Their linemen controlled the line offensively and defensively. They had pretty good special guys and running backs. They were bigger and stronger and dominating. They would run the ball and might pass every now and then. They were physical, very physical."

And even 20 years later, into the turn of the century, the Nebraska offensive line was still ferocious with such standouts as center Dominic Raiola and guards Russ Hochstein and Toniu Fonoti with the San Diego Chargers, Minnesota Vikings and Miami Dolphins. All three have had careers in the NFL.

"Nebraska was basically an NFL feeder for offensive linemen," said Duke Revard, an MU linebacker from 1998 to 2001. "They were all 330 and could run. Your only hope was to not let them touch you. I don't think there was a close second in terms of phys-icalness. Texas could have been. They had two tackles who were, like, 370 in 2000. They are both in the NFL. Texas played half the time like they didn't want to get their uniform dirty. They were huge physical specimens. But they just didn't have a lot scrap in them. They were more finesse. They were All-Americans who didn't feel the need to be scrappy."

The Walk-on Phenomenon

During its heyday under Osborne and later Frank Solich, Nebraska's walk-on program would allow the Cornhuskers to have four practice stations instead of just the two the normal program would have. Nebraska could get twice the work done in a practice.

"I think we had what was the best walk-on program in the country," said Solich. "We had a large number of people on our team. We would have two offensive teams running plays at one time and two defensive teams running plays at the same time. We just gave more people more reps and were able to develop some of those guys who walked on and weren't able to step in and play right away. They had some talent and they just kept working, working, working. By the time they were juniors and seniors, they were not only backup players, we had some who were starting. And that was a big advantage."

Walk-on players such as Brainard, Nebraska, fullback Joel Makovicka (1995–1998) and his fullback brother, Jeff (1992–1995), often have been scouted in Cornhuskers camps and at high school games. Joel went on to play in the NFL with the Arizona Cardinals.

"They treat you like any other athlete," said Joel Makovicka. "I was recruited out of high school, so maybe I was treated a little better. But they treat you pretty much the same. Those guys [walk-ons] come in and maybe are not as mature, but they will help by their junior or senior year. That really helps Nebraska football."

"It is like Coach Osborne says, you need numbers," said Minter. "In order to build a great team, you need numbers. You can't do it with 80-some guys. You need numbers to practice against because one day you are going to need them. And so our walk-on program was huge. Those guys understood, maybe their fourth year being in college they would get a chance to play. They knew their role. And I think to be a great team you have to have everybody understand roles."

Steve Pederson, in a 1996 interview when he was the director of NU football operations, explained, "Everybody gets a lot of repetitions, and that causes them to be better players. I think they know the best 22 players here are going to play. It doesn't matter if you walked on here and nobody had ever heard of you or you were the most recruited guy. And it creates competition among all of them, too. If you are a wide receiver, you really can't afford to dog it in a couple of practices because there is some guy who wants to play so bad he can't stand it, and he is going to press you and press you, so you need to perform every day."

The Cornhuskers have had some notable walk-ons from distant places, such as running back I.M. Hipp from South Carolina, defensive end Jimmy Williams, and his brother Toby, a tackle, both from Washington, D.C. Jimmy Williams is one of a handful of walk-ons to achieve All-America honors. He then later went on to a long professional career.

"Jimmy Williams hit me in 1980, my sophomore year," said former Kansas State quarterback Darrell Dickey. "He caught me under my shoulder pads like he was shot out of cannon. He broke three of my ribs. He made initial contact at the 5. I got rid of the ball. He hit me so hard, he knocked me two yards deep in the end zone. I walked off, and I was done for the day."

The walk-on poster child, as far as offensive linemen are concerned, may be Adam Treu, who grew up in Lincoln and went to games with his father as a kid. He was a 6'6", 230-pound freshmen when he walked on the Nebraska football team in the early 1990s and paid for his first season.

"And then I was offered a scholarship," Treu said in 1996. "History shows that a good percentage of the players who come in [as walk-ons] actually play and start. Another driving force is you want to show the coaches and show everybody you are a quality player, and walking on doesn't mean you're a ragamuffin. Everybody has a chance. Some are better than others. The way you work in the weight room or out in the field in practices greatly improves your stock.

"They will take a guy like myself, a guy who will be a project," Treu said. "They say, 'He has the frame. He will get on the weights extensively and he will fill out.' That's how a lot of the linemen are. They just have to wait their turn."

Treu finished his Nebraska playing days five years later at 6'6", 300 pounds and went on the play in the NFL with the Oakland Raiders for a decade, from 1997 to 2006, and played in a Super Bowl.

Besides the obvious benefits on the field, Nebraska's walk-ons have created a sense of state pride

"I understand the walk-ons now more than I ever understood it before than when I lived in Omaha," said Aaron Taylor. "Now I live in rural Nebraska [in North Platte]. These people live and die by what goes on up there at the stadium. I hear people in North Platte still talking about kids who played at Nebraska back in the 1970s. 'Yeah, we had Steve who played for Nebraska, I think in 1972 to 1974.' It doesn't matter if you were a scholarship athlete or a walk-on, they truly cherish that. And it brings a sense of community. It brings a sense of support to the athletics department."

"The majority of walk-ons are from Nebraska," Steve Pederson said in a 1996 interview. "You have those I.M. Hipp stories. But those are fewer and further between than reality. Most of them are Nebraska kids who have dreamed about playing here and are walking on."

Nebraska's Adoring Fans

Taylor remembers his going turkey-hunting in Valentine, Nebraska, in the middle of the Sand Hills. It is a desolate area of the state where he and his companion, offensive guard Brandt Wade, drove for two and a half hours and didn't see a town or a car, just sand hills.

"We are pumping gas and we go inside to get a Coke or something and pay," Taylor said. "And you had six or so farmers sitting around. And you know how everybody turns around and looks at you. You are the new guy in town, who the hell are you? They turned and we were paying.

"And one of the old farmers speaks up and says, 'Aren't you Aaron Taylor from Nebraska?' And I said, 'Yes, sir.'

"And another guy goes, 'You are Brandt Wade from Springfield, Nebraska, aren't you?' This guy is a third-team guy. We are five and a half hours from Lincoln, and these guys know who our third-teamers are. They said, 'We thank you for everything you are doing.' Our comment was, 'We hope we are making you proud. We are going turkey-hunting.' 'Well, good luck,' they said.

"That is the way it is. People at Nebraska, they don't talk about the first-team players. They say, 'What do you think about Joe Blow sitting second on the depth chart? Do you think that guy who is third-team right tackle is going to make a move? He has the frame and is putting on some weight. Do you think he will be able to contribute?' They love it."

As a result, Nebraska has perhaps the most enduring fan base of perhaps any team in college football. Through the 2007 season, Nebraska has played before 289 consecutive sellouts.

And from the Devaney through the Solich eras—a period of little more than 40 years—the coaching staff kept in touch with the fan base from one end of the state to the other.

"All these little towns, whether there are 200 people, or 2,000 people, or 20,000 people, these guys know a John Melton, a George Darlington, a Milt Tenopir, Dan Young, Charlie McBride," said Aaron Taylor. "They have all sat there and had dinner with them, or had a beer with them, or whatever and become friends with these people over the years. Osborne's staff would reach out to the state. And they would get to know the individuals, get to know the coaches, get to know the players. All the schools in Nebraska ran the same offense and defense."

At Memorial Stadium, many of those Nebraskans migrate to Lincoln on football Saturdays in the fall. "Nebraska fans respect the game and most of the fans understand what it takes to play the game," Fiala said. "They look at our team, they look at the other team, and they know the kind of work it takes, the kind of diligence it takes to play, the kind of work ethic our kids have. And they kind of move that over to the other team, and they appreciate what the team has done, be it a win or loss. They fully understand it.

"I think this already got started with Florida State and Bobby Bowden in 1980. He advised his team to wear their helmets when they walked off the field because they didn't know what sort of treatment they were going to get with respect to the Nebraska fans. And he said, much to his amazement, when we walked off the field the Nebraska fans were applauding us. That's really the first major recognition. That's when he became a fan of our program and a fan of Tom's, because of the fans. He even wrote a letter to the newspaper recognizing the fans, thanking them, and saying how he would have a special place in his heart for Nebraska fans."

A year later Penn State came to Lincoln and pulled out a 30–24 victory behind quarterback Todd Blackledge and tailback Curt Warner.

"That was my first time ever going to Lincoln," Blackledge said. "And I had heard about their fans. And it was incredible. It was a back-and-forth game. I remember our field-goal kicker kicked five field goals. We won by six points. I remember when we came off the field after the game, right by the tunnel there, all the fans there stood and clapped for us. It was the most incredible thing I had seen as far as their respect for us and Joe Paterno."

chapter 12
The Solich Years

Frank Solich leads his players onto the field to play against Arizona State in the Black Coaches Association Classic game August 24, 2002, at Memorial Stadium.

The cornerstone player of the Frank Solich years was Nebraska's third Heisman Trophy winner, quarterback Eric Crouch. In many ways, the success Solich had during his tenure was tied to Crouch, who began a four-year reign as the Nebraska signal-caller in Solich's first season as head coach in 1998.

The defending national champions won their first five games of the 1998 season, rolling along until a narrow 24–17 victory over Oklahoma State at Arrowhead Stadium in Kansas City in game number five. It was a Cowboys home game moved to Kansas City for a big payday. And it looked more like a Nebraska home game with the red-clad fans in a majority of the crowd of 79,555.

Nevertheless, the following week would begin Nebraska's rude introduction to Texas A&M football at College Station. And three games later the Cornhuskers would have a re-introduction to Texas football. For the first time in the new Big 12 Conference of rotating schedules, Nebraska would play the Aggies and Longhorns in regular-season games. Nebraska already had seen the athletic ability of Texas in a 37–27 defeat in the first Big 12 Conference title game in 1996, which cost the Cornhuskers a chance at the national title.

The first loss of the Solich era was a 28–21 defeat to the Aggies in College Station. The second loss was a 20–16 defeat to Texas in Lincoln. A third conference loss to Kansas State, 40–30, sent the Cornhuskers to a second-place finish behind the Wildcats in the Big 12 North Division.

It was the Cornhuskers' first loss to Kansas State since a 12–0 defeat to the Wildcats in Lincoln in 1968.

"When Tom Osborne left my redshirt freshman year, you could tell something happened," Crouch said. "There wasn't quite the leadership there. We went 9–4, and it was, like, the most devastating thing that had ever happened at Nebraska. For us, it was like part of the state had died. Everyone was depressed. Sales went down for merchandise. It was a bad deal for a lot of businesses out there. But we got back on track. We had some guys who were seniors who left, and we started building some good leadership. The class that was ahead of my class, we had a lot of great players. It wasn't a great big shakeup. Solich had been there for 19 years. Milt Tenopir, Dan Young, Ron Brown, and Charlie McBride, all those guys had been there for so long. It was not like the program had died or anything. But Osborne was a big part of the success of that program."

The four losses by Nebraska in a 9–4 season were the most by a Nebraska team since Devaney's 1968 club finished 6–4 on the way to a fourth-place tie in the old Big 8. While it was not apparent at the time—because Nebraska bounced back with 12-, 10-, and 11-victory seasons the next three years—it demonstrated Nebraska's vulnerability to a much tougher league with the Texas schools involved.

Crouch's Recruitment, Promise

But as a redshirt freshman, Crouch had shown great promise, rushing and passing for 1,060 yards in 1998. The Omaha Millard North product had stayed in state after spurning offers from Notre Dame coach Lou Holtz and Ohio State coach John Cooper. Holtz was out of Notre Dame before Crouch even played at Nebraska; Cooper was gone from Ohio State by the time Crouch used up his eligibility at Nebraska and graduated; and Osborne only stuck around for the 1997 season when Crouch was redshirted.

"Ohio State wanted me as their slash player—slot back, defensive back, receiver, punt returner," Crouch said. "They didn't know [what position I would play]. They just recruited me as an athlete. I wasn't really prepared for that. In my mind, I knew what I wanted to be. I took a visit to Notre Dame. Lou Holtz was the coach there. And they were kind of telling me the same thing. Dave Roberts was the quarterback coach then [at Notre Dame]. He said, 'We want you as a quarterback, but we are not 100 percent that is where you would stay.' So I came back to Nebraska, but I had three scholarship offers on the table before my senior year. Nebraska was the one at the time that didn't have any questions about where I would play."

Osborne had been a part of the staff that had recruited Crouch, and the NU staff had promised Crouch he would get a shot at quarterback. Once there, he became only the third quarterback in major-college history at the time to rush for 3,000 yards and pass for 4,000 yards in a career. His great career was capped off by a Heisman Trophy in 2001, when he also won the Davey O'Brien (for best quarterback) and Walter Camp Player of the Year awards.

Nebraska's four-year record with Crouch at the helm was 42–9, a better than 80 percent winning percentage. That's excellent. The problem was Nebraska's four-year record with Crouch post-Osborne suffered in comparison to Osborne's final four seasons, when the Cornhuskers won three national titles and were 49–2—truly a golden period in Nebraska football. During Crouch's four years, the Cornhuskers won the Big 12 once and took two North Division titles and split four bowl games.

Yet he was a such a unique player, that the Nebraska coaching staff couldn't resist centering the offense around him.

"I have such great respect for him," Solich said in 2007. "He had immense talent. And so we ended up putting the ball in his hands because of his talent. And he was the best player. He was the best running back. He was the best quarterback. And he probably was the best receiver. And you could line him up for kick returns. And you could not get him off the field. His toughness—he took more and more hits, but just kept coming back. He certainly earned the Heisman. I think he was the best player in the country that year."

While Aaron Taylor has great respect for Crouch, he also pointed out that the Cornhuskers may have relied on him too much.

"I think they got away from true Nebraska football," Taylor said. "I would dare any Nebraska fan to name me an I-back during Eric Crouch's years. I know who they were—Dahrran Diedrick and Dan Alexander. No one else has said this. And it is my own personal opinion. And it takes nothing away from Crouch as a player or as an individual, or is a knock on his character or anything. But I think it was a little bit of downturn in Nebraska football when he was quarterback because they relied on his athletic ability so much.

"We were 'I-back U.' And now all of a sudden we weren't developing I-backs during his four years. We were relying on him so much, we got away from what I call true Nebraska football—running the option, running the isolation play, running the fullback trap, running the off-tackle plays, running the play-action passes. If you look at the plays being run during his tenure versus the 15 years prior to Eric Crouch, you will see a completely different offense. It was not Eric Crouch's fault. But it was the lack of development of a true I-back. We had guys who were starting at I-back who should have been backups and third-stringers during his years."

The next season after Crouch left, Solich's fifth season, when the program should have been strong, the Cornhuskers dropped to 7–7.

Ricky Williams, Texas Provide Tough Hurdles

In Crouch's freshman year, 1998, Nebraska had a 47–game home winning streak when Texas came to town on Halloween. The Cornhuskers had not lost a game in Lincoln since the 1991 season, a 36–21 decision to fourth-ranked Washington. But here, again, the toughness of the Big 12 and the competitive nature of such programs as Texas, Texas A&M, and Texas Tech surfaced.

Texas was looking for a signature road victory in Mack Brown's first season in Austin. And running back Ricky Williams needed a solid rushing game against a top team to enhance his Heisman Trophy chances. The Longhorns accomplished both in a stirring 20–16 night victory when Texas quarterback Major Applewhite connected on a clutch two-yard pass on third down to Wane McGarity with 2:47 remaining. Nebraska lost to an unranked opponent at home for the first time since the 1978 season against Missouri (35–31).

Williams was a huge factor in the game. He rushed for 150 yards, the most by an opposing running back in Lincoln in a decade. Oklahoma State's Barry Sanders piled up 189 yards in a 63–42 loss to Nebraska in 1988 on the way to the Heisman Trophy.

Before the game, Nebraska defenders said they were going to make Williams a target. Unfazed, Williams said, "I'm going to make them the target when I get the ball."

"I asked Ricky why he said it," Brown revealed later. "He said, 'I want our team to be confident. If they don't think I'm confident, then they won't be confident.'"

Williams showed his toughness when he made a touchdown-saving tackle on an interception and also caught a blitzing linebacker with a block on a big Applewhite pass. After the game, Nebraska fans applauded him, as did Nebraska defensive coordinator Charlie McBride.

"The guy is something special," McBride said. "The two best guys we have played against are Barry Sanders and Ricky Williams. If he doesn't win the Heisman Trophy, college football has something wrong with it. It's the politically right thing to do. He is such a power kid and has such great balance. And you have other things you like, not football things—his work habits and him staying for his senior year when he could have made a lot of money."

Williams wound up winning the 1998 Heisman Trophy and became the leading career rusher in major-college history before his record was broken by Wisconsin's Ron Dayne a year later.

Nebraska's only loss during the 12–1 1999 season was to Texas, when Applewhite rallied the Longhorns to a 24–20 victory in Austin for their third-straight victory over the Cornhuskers. But Nebraska got a measure of revenge by dominating the Longhorns 22–6 in the 1999 Big 12 title game in San Antonio when the Blackshirts held Texas without a touchdown for the first time since the 1985 season. Nebraska allowed Texas just nine yards rushing on 29 carries and advanced as Big 12 champion to the Fiesta Bowl.

McBride Steps Down

Following the 1999 season, one of the longtime defensive pillars of the Nebraska football dynasty was gone—just as Tom Osborne was two years previously.

A 31–21 victory over Tennessee in the 29th annual Fiesta Bowl would signal the final game of Charlie McBride's coaching career in an emotion-filled night in the desert. It was truly the passing of an era. It was also the final game for Nebraska's senior safety, Mike Brown, who would go on to a pro football career with the Chicago Bears. Brown was an All-American his senior season of 1999.

"He was kind of crying a little bit because it is over for him," Brown said of McBride after the game. "He has been doing this for so long. He is going to move into a new chapter in his life. He's a tremendous coach. He has so much respect on this team. He's just someone that puts his heart into what he does. His players try to give their heart right back to him. He is going to be missed. We love him dearly."

McBride, in his 37th year of college coaching, did not broadcast that the Fiesta Bowl would be his final game.

"It's not his style to tell people that he's retiring so they play for him," Brown continued. "That's the type of person he is. He just went about it quietly. He has always been hurt in his knees, back. It's sad to see him leave. But I'm also happy that he's going to be able to enjoy his life."

McBride started his assistant coaching career at Arizona State. He arrived at Nebraska in 1977, when Tom Osborne was a young head coach of the Cornhuskers, and spent 23 years on the Cornhuskers staff, the final two under coach Frank Solich.

"My first win was when I was coaching with Frank Kush in this stadium, and my last win was here, too," McBride said. "That meant so much to me."

From 1977 to 1999, Nebraska produced dozens of all-conference defensive players under McBride. The Cornhuskers led the country in 1984 in total defense and scoring defense and in 1981 in pass defense. And they were often ranked in the top 10 in those categories during McBride's tenure.

"Certainly, Coach McBride is known around the country as one of the great and maybe as great a defensive coordinator as there is," Solich said. "I know that we would not trade him for anybody....His players always have played very hard for him. There's a reason why Nebraska has had great defensive football teams over the years. Coach McBride is that reason."

"Their defensive coordinator, Charlie McBride, could make the slightest adjustment, and the other team would have to completely change their offense," said Steve Hatchell, a longtime observer of Nebraska football in the Big 8 and Big 12 Conferences.

Safety Mike Minter saluted McBride in 2007 when he said, "I think the main thing that Coach McBride brought to the game was passion. He made you want to run through a wall. That is the biggest thing I think he brought because I think that is what coaching is. Coaching is getting your players to believe in what you are saying. And he did a great job of doing that."

Notre Dame Game in 2000

At the beginning of the 2000 season, Nebraska was atop the national polls by virtue of its 1999 12–1 finish and the fact that Crouch and several others were returning. After a season-opening 49–13 victory over San Jose State in Lincoln, the game everybody had been waiting for arrived: Nebraska–Notre Dame in South Bend.

Nebraska and Notre Dame had not played since the 1973 Orange Bowl, Bob Devaney's final game, when Johnny Rodgers put the exclamation point on his Heisman Trophy–winning season in a 40–6 Cornhuskers victory. The two teams had not played in South Bend since 1947.

"That game was being talked about for two years before we played it," Crouch said. "That was all anybody was talking about. The Four Horsemen, the tradition Notre Dame had. We couldn't wait to get on the field to play it. I just remember it brought a lot of media surrounding that game. I think there were

Eric Crouch runs for a touchdown to give the Huskers a memorable 27–24 overtime win against Notre Dame on September 9, 2000, in South Bend, Indiana.

thousands and thousands of people standing outside that game—Nebraska fans.

"When I came outside to the Notre Dame Stadium, [Fighting Irish] fans had sold their tickets. There was a lot of red in that stadium. I remember Notre Dame being very upset with their own people for doing that. We jumped on them, and it was 21–0, and they returned two kicks, and before you knew it, it was 21–21. And it went into overtime, and we wound up winning the game."

As would be the case, during his years at Nebraska, Crouch was the center of the winning play in a 27–24 overtime victory before 80,232 fans at Notre Dame Stadium.

"The winning score was really a trap play where I had a couple of lead blockers," Crouch said. "We loaded the defense down with our fullback, and we had three running backs in our backfield—like the wishbone. So I faked to the fullback and I led the blockers outside. To have those guys blocking and to score that touchdown at Notre Dame, especially in overtime—a lot of people ask me what is the favorite play of your career, and that is it. It was such a big game. It was a highlight of my career."

Crouch Wins 2001 Heisman, Other Awards

In his senior season, Crouch led Nebraska to 11 straight victories during the tragedy-marred 2001 season when 9/11 actually postponed the Rice game for five days. After picking up easy victories over TCU and Troy State, the Cornhuskers beat Notre Dame 27–10 before topping Rice 48–3 in a lightning-interrupted game as well.

The Cornhuskers, at 4–0, didn't venture out of the state of Nebraska until playing at Missouri on September 29. The previous season, Missouri had been more competitive in a 42–24 loss in Lincoln. And this was a tight game early against the Tigers, who were starting to make a move under coach Gary Pinkel. Nebraska, in fact, would not win another game at Missouri in the next three tries, losing in Columbia in 2003, 2005, and 2007.

Deep in Missouri territory in the 2001 game, Crouch made the play that turned the game around and placed his name in the Cornhuskers record books with the longest rushing play in school history—95 yards.

"It was third and seven and we were on the 5-yard line," Crouch said. "And we were trying to throw an out route. I rolled out and ended up about seven yards deep in our end zone. And the game was pretty close. It was a big turning point of the game. It was at their place, and they always play us tough. That was the best time in that game to turn things around.

"I zig-zagged a little bit—if you want to add that up, it was over 100 yards," Crouch added. "I almost got sacked in the end zone for a safety. A guy grabbed me and kind of pulled at my jersey. I started to kind of fall, I broke that tackle, and the rest is history."

The Cornhuskers pulled away for a 36–3 victory. And Crouch had another clip for his personal Heisman Trophy highlight film.

In 2001 Nebraska had a trio of 10-point home victories over Texas Tech, Oklahoma, and Kansas State, and entered a regular-season-ending showdown with Colorado in Boulder with an 11–0 record and a number-two rating. Nebraska was expected to handle the Buffaloes and meet Oklahoma in a rematch for the Big 12 title at Texas Stadium. But neither made it. Oklahoma lost to Oklahoma State, and the Cornhuskers fell to Colorado 62–36. It was the most points at the time ever given up by a Nebraska team.

Still, Crouch cemented his Heisman Trophy chances with a brilliant performance against Colorado with a then-school-record 360 yards (198 yards passing and 162 yards rushing). A week later he was named the best quarterback in the country, and two days after that the best player when he took the Heisman.

"When I won the Davey O'Brien Award my senior year," Crouch said, "I thought this is a great honor because not only was

Eric Crouch won the 2001 Heisman after a spectacular season running and throwing the ball.

he a quarterback, he had a lot of versatility. That is what my game has been all about—and having a winning attitude and being very committed. And I think that is exactly how he was.

"In a lot of ways, there were a lot of people who were very deserving of the [Heisman Trophy] that year," Crouch said in 2007. "There were four quarterbacks—Joey Harrington [Oregon], Ken Dorsey [Miami], Rex Grossman [Florida]—and all of those guys a couple of years later were starters in the NFL."

Like O'Brien, who was adept at running or passing or catching, Crouch could do it all. His senior season, Crouch completed 55.6 percent of his passes for 1,510 yards and seven touchdowns. He rushed for an additional 1,115 yards and 18 touchdowns. He accounted for 218.8 yards a game.

Crouch's Heisman Trophy—winning season ended on a sour note when the Cornhuskers dropped their second straight game, a 37–14 defeat to top-ranked Miami in the Rose Bowl. Despite the loss to Colorado, Nebraska had maintained a number-two spot in the BCS standings behind Miami and earned a second trip to the Rose Bowl. It was the first time for Nebraska in the Rose Bowl since the Cornhuskers had played Stanford following the 1940 season.

Solich Falls Out of Favor

The defensive collapse in the final two games of the 2001 season—giving up a total of 99 points to Colorado and Miami—did not portend good things in 2002. With Crouch gone, Nebraska still easily won its first three games of the season at home against Arizona State, Troy State, and Utah State.

But then came disastrous road losses to unranked Penn State (40–7) and number 19 Iowa State (36–14). After the two lopsided losses, for the first time since the fifth week of the 1981 season, Nebraska was not ranked in the Associated Press top 25 poll. The Cornhuskers had been ranked an incredible 348 straight weeks over 22 seasons.

Nebraska was in a free fall and would only win three league games, finishing fourth in the Big 12 North Division, ahead of Missouri and Kansas, two teams the Cornhuskers had long winning streaks over. A 7–6 regular-season finish resulted in a 7–7 final record–Nebraska's most losses since 1958–when the Cornhuskers fell to Mississippi in the Independence Bowl.

A particularly damaging loss was a 49–13 bashing at Kansas State. It was Solich's third loss to the Wildcats in five years and began to emphasize the fact Nebraska was slipping in the conference.

Solich was faced with a decision to revamp his staff or possibly suffer the consequences from new athletics director, 45-year-old Steve Pederson, who took over on December 20, 2002. Pederson succeeded Bill Byrne, who had left for the same position at Texas A&M.

A Nebraska graduate, Pederson had been Osborne's administrative assistant from 1982 to 1986, then made stops at football powerhouses Ohio State and Tennessee before serving as Nebraska's director of football operations for Osborne from 1994 to 1996. He left to become the athletics director of Pittsburgh. But what he returned to was quite different from Nebraska's national-title-caliber program in the old Big 8.

Adrian Fiala, the former player and current era radio personality, said Solich might have become a victim of being too loyal to his staff. When Bob Devaney retired after the 1972 season, Osborne retained much of the staff.

"He wanted to keep basically the staff intact," Fiala said of Solich when Osborne retired after the 1997 season. "And he did. Maybe that was a little bit of his undoing. There were times when things weren't going so well. Up through 1999 (12–1) and 2000 (10–2) things progressed pretty well. If changes were going to be made, though, they probably should have been made at that time versus waiting. And then you know what happened after that."

While Nebraska's defense was becoming porous and starting to look slow, its offense lacked punch. The passing game lacked imagination. One Missouri player believed the physical nature of the program also was gone.

"Nebraska in 1997 and 1998 had it. In 1999 they had it," Missouri linebacker Duke Revard (1998–2001) said. "By 2000 they were losing it. In 2001 they were losing it. They weren't the same physical team. I don't think they had the same physical players."

Solich stands by his decision after the 2002 season of replacing longtime coaches Milt Tenopir (1974–2002), George Darlington (1973–2002), and Dan Young (1983–2002), and also some shorter-timers.

"I feel comfortable about what I got done at Nebraska," said Solich, who had a 58–19 record (75.3 percent winning percentage) and one Big 12 title. "It is obvious that expectations are always going to be very, very high at that level of football. I took over a coaching staff that was intact. I had to make some moves on the coaching staff. I think those were playing out. The staff did age. And I thought the moves that were made [were working]."

Solich's staff changes may have gotten him another season. But it also caused friction within the Cornhuskers family.

"When Milt Tenopir got fired, I was sticking up for my coach and someone I thought was very, very important for me and made a few comments that I shouldn't have made to the paper," Aaron Taylor said.

Taylor was attending a welcoming party for Pederson after the assistant-coaching changes and met up with Solich, who had been an assistant while Taylor was playing.

"Solich was across the room, and we made eye contact, but I just kept looking somewhere else," Taylor said. "I was thinking to myself, 'I hope he didn't see me.' I thought, 'Oh, he is walking this way. He can't be coming to see me.' This is all going though my head. Then the next thing I know he wants to talk to me. He made the comment to me he understands how I feel. And I am welcome at the stadium any time that I want to come up to practice, to meetings or any of that. He understands the comments I made in the paper. And that is one of the good things about being a coach, that you have those kinds of relationships with players, they will go to bat for you anytime. It was one of those deals I didn't want to be confronted by him. He understood where I was coming from. He understood I shouldn't have said what I said. And he could have handled things in a different way. But we still wanted one thing: what was best for Nebraska football."

In Solich's final season of 2003, the Cornhuskers won their first five games, but then came a 41–24 loss at Missouri, the Tigers' first victory over the Cornhuskers since 1978. The Cornhuskers were hammered at Texas, 31–7, and blistered in Lincoln, 38–9, by Kansas State, which won the North Division by a game over the Cornhuskers. That dreary defeat before a nearly empty stadium except for the small Kansas State contingent spelled the near end for Solich.

"It started snowing, and I was there at the end of the game," said former Kansas State tight end Eddy Whitley of remaining in the stands while all the Nebraska fans were leaving. "It was one of the proudest moments I have ever had. I am still a blueblood Kansas State fan, and that is a way of revenge for me because I never beat them."

After a 31–22 victory over Colorado in the 2003 regular-season finale, Solich, who posted a 9–3 regular-season record, was out. His defensive coordinator, Bo Pelini, who would return as the Cornhuskers' head coach after the completion of the 2007 season, coached the 2003 Alamo Bowl victory over Michigan State.

Solich's offense at Nebraska was outdated, his critics said. Solich said it was pragmatic to run the offense that he ran with the Cornhuskers.

Solich, who has been the head football coach at Ohio University the last three seasons, observed, "The bottom line is you have to be utilizing the personnel you have. We had great personnel at Nebraska to pound the ball at you, run some options, and throw some play-action passes off of it."

Solich has been doing a solid job with the Bobcats—19–18, in three seasons—with one division title and one bowl appearance at a program that had four straight losing seasons before he arrived.

"I think he has done little different things [at Ohio]," said Western Michigan coach Bill Cubit. "But his core, his values are the same: win with good defense, his special teams are outstanding, and offensively they maybe aren't going to beat you throwing the ball, but they run and get ahead of you, and they are tough to beat."

From 1962 to 2003, a period of 42 years, that formula tended to work. Nebraska didn't have a losing season. But that might have been tough for Solich to sustain if he had stayed on in Lincoln.

"I don't think you will see many teams have dynasties of 10- and 20-year runs of winning nine games every year," said Buffalo coach Turner Gill, who was a player and an assistant coach at Nebraska. "Nebraska had 33 years of winning at least nine games a season. I don't think you will see that happen anymore."

Gill says the NCAA mandated reduction to 85 total football scholarships for major-college programs has spread the talent around.

"And coaching-wise, I don't think some of the coaches will hang around that long before going on to the next level, the NFL," Gill added. "They may stay at a school five years. And assistant coaches leave schools quicker now. At Nebraska, nobody would leave."

"When we moved to the Big 12, yeah, I think it makes it difficult because the conference becomes a whole lot better," said Aaron Taylor. "The difficult thing for us is you are not going to win all the time. You are not going to play for the national championship like we did in the 1990s. We all understand that was a special time we all went through. But there is no reason you can't compete and you can't play hard."

Why did Nebraska football slip? There are several theories. Here are some of them:

- Solich did not have the recruiting power that Osborne did. Often cited was the imposing size of Osborne walking into a home or a room of alumni and/or supporters and commanding a presence. Despite the early picking at Osborne for his close losses in the 1970s and failures against Oklahoma, he became an icon by winning big bowl games and national championships. The much shorter Solich would walk into a room, and if it was crowded, nobody would even notice. He never won a national title.

• The entrance into the Big 12 Conference finally caught up with Nebraska. Texas, Texas A&M, and Texas Tech provided stiffer competition on the field. Plus, Nebraska could no longer offer Texas high school recruits an alternative to the Southwest Conference because it had disbanded, and the three most powerful schools, plus Baylor, were playing in the same league as Nebraska. In 1996 and 1997 Osborne played Texas once in his final two seasons—in the 1996 title game—and lost. He beat Texas A&M in the 1997 Big 12 title game. Osborne was 4–0 against Baylor and Texas Tech in 1996 and 1997. Likewise, Solich was 4–0 against Baylor and Texas Tech, but was 4–5 against Texas and A&M from 1998 to 2003.

• Nebraska had enjoyed a facilities edge over several programs in the old Big 8. But the improvement of facilities at Kansas State, Colorado, and eventually Missouri and Kansas made those programs more competitive. The Cornhuskers' winning streak against Kansas State (dating to 1968) ended in 1998, and over the last decade Nebraska has only broken even against the Wildcats. Nebraska's winning streak over Missouri (dating to 1978), ended in 2003, and Nebraska is 2–3 against Missouri in the last five years. Nebraska's winning streak over Kansas (from a 21–17 victory in 1969) ended with a 40–15 loss in 2005, Callahan's second season. This past season, Kansas pummeled Nebraska with the most points ever against the Cornhuskers.

• And finally, with the formation of the Big 12, Nebraska no longer could recruit or admit nonqualifiers as it could in the old Big 8. This eliminated a pool of players who would have starred at Nebraska as they did in the mid-1990s under Osborne when he won three national titles.

Sources close to the program said that Nebraska chancellor in the mid-1990s, Graham Spanier, now the president at Penn State, was told by Osborne not to allow the other Big 12 presidents to change the academic requirements for players' entrance into the league from the Big 8 standards. But this was a non-starter for Texas, which threatened to go to the Pac-10 Conference if the tougher entrance requirements were not enacted. They were. "Tom said it was a killer [for Nebraska football]," one source said.

"Coach Osborne was big about getting individuals to college and graduate," Taylor said. "Jared Tomich was a Prop 48. You basically come in, you are on scholarship, you have nothing to do with the team, all you do is go to school and work on academics. I wouldn't say becoming eligible, but I think that is what it is. We had a lot of individuals. Jared Tomich was dyslexic. And he had a speech problem and all these things. He ended up overcoming it. Coach Osborne loved to help individuals like that succeed."

Meanwhile, after firing Solich, Pederson would make the decision on the next coach, who would veer away from all of those values. Nebraska went outside the family for the first time in decades for its head football coach. And Nebraska football would pay dearly for it.

What made this particularly troubling to some Nebraska observers was the fact Solich had overhauled his staff and had put together a pretty good defensive staff.

"You had Bo Pelini, Marvin Sanders, Jimmy Williams—a lot of guys who were damn good coaches," Taylor said. "He goes in and fires them after a year. Those guys took a defense that was [average] and they took it up to 11th in the nation [in total defense]."

chapter 13
Callahan Years Lead to Pelini

Nebraska's new football coach Bo Pelini is introduced by athletics director Tom Osborne at a news conference in Lincoln on December 2, 2007.

The switch to coach Bill Callahan in January 2004 would signal the unraveling of Nebraska's football culture. For the first time in more than 40 years there would be no ties to Bob Devaney in Lincoln.

Steve Pederson, who had grown up in the previous culture as a student, sports information assistant, director of football operations, and finally athletics director, opted for an NFL head coach without any Nebraska ties.

The fact Nebraska could not snap its fingers and hire a coach was upsetting to some former players and alumni. But it also demonstrated that many in the coaching fraternity wondered what it would be like to work for Pederson, who fired a coach who had won 75 percent of his games.

"It was a 41-day process, where he tried to hire Houston Nutt from Arkansas, when he tried to hire Mike Zimmer [assistant coach] from the Dallas Cowboys," said Aaron Taylor. "He tried hiring a few people and he kept getting 'no.' What the hell was going on? Then he would have press conference on top of press conference. There was no rhyme or reason to what the hell he was doing. He started off on the wrong foot, the way he fired that staff. Whether Solich should have been there or not, he had put together a good staff. And he put together a damn good defensive staff."

New Cornhuskers coach Bill Callahan was only two years removed from leading the Oakland Raiders to the Super Bowl. He showed he could handle Xs and Os. But now he had to unite one state behind one program, as Devaney had done starting in the early 1960s. And he failed miserably. He went about changing everything.

His background was completely foreign to Cornhuskers football.

Callahan was 47 years old when he took the Nebraska head job. A native of Chicago and a quarterback at Illinois Benedictine College from 1975 to 1977, Callahan, after two seasons as a high school assistant, spent 15 seasons as a college assistant at Illinois (1980–1986), Northern Arizona (1987–1988), Southern Illinois (1989), and Wisconsin (1990–1994). For three seasons,

Callahan was offensive line coach for the Philadelphia Eagles before four seasons as the Oakland Raiders offensive coordinator. He became head coach of the Raiders in 2002 and had a 17–18 two-year record, losing to Tampa Bay in the Super Bowl after the 2002 season.

"You didn't break the chain Bob started in 1962," said Jim Walden, who was an assistant coach under Devaney. "That has led to problems they have today. Bill Callahan didn't understand how strong the ties were to Bob Devaney. It started with Frankie Solich leaving. Things were always run a certain way. And there was a certain dignity to what had been started by Devaney. All of a sudden it was not there. It is a big mistake. When you try to fix something that isn't broken, you get yourself in trouble."

From the run-oriented offense that Osborne built and nurtured, the Cornhuskers switched to the much more pass-oriented West Coast offense. Callahan would minimize the walk-on program and cast aside relationships with many of the past players, who called this the "professionalization" of the Nebraska program.

Whether or not Solich could have stopped the bleeding of the 2004 season (5–6) or beyond is debatable. But history tells us that Solich's problems were nothing compared to the hemorrhaging that eventually occurred in 2007. Callahan's and Pederson's failure to understand the Nebraska culture compounded already aforementioned developing problems.

Callahan's first season of 2004 ended with a 5–6 record. And for the first time since 1961, the year before Devaney arrived, Nebraska was not in a bowl game. On October 9, 2004, Nebraska gave up 70 points to Texas Tech. At that point, 70 points was the most allowed in school history. Nebraska lost its final three games to Iowa State, Oklahoma, and Colorado. The 26–20 regular-season-ending loss to Colorado in Lincoln cost Nebraska a spot in the Fort Worth Bowl. That's what it had come to with Nebraska football, needing and not getting a victory over an unranked Colorado in the final game of the season to go to a bowl.

Callahan's Cornhuskers won only one more conference game in 2005 than they did in 2004 to get to four league victories.

And in his first two seasons Callahan had a 13–10 overall record. He had to win the last three games of the 2005 season to even get that far. Only a thrilling 32–28 victory over Michigan in the 2005 Alamo Bowl allowed the season to really end on a positive note.

At the time, Nebraska's performance was more or less considered to be part of the process of Callahan recruiting his players and putting his system in place. And when Nebraska won the Big 12 North in 2006, Callahan reflected on the accomplishment prior to playing Auburn, and losing to the Tigers, in the Cotton Bowl. Nebraska lost the Big 12 title game to Oklahoma.

"It has taken some time to put the pieces in place to be successful," Callahan said of a 9-win 2006 season. "And it has happened over the course of three years. We had some ups and downs in that first year, that transitional year, and it came to fruition at the end of last season, and now this season was a plus."

Nebraska's offensive coordinator at the time, Jay Norvell, said the Cornhuskers needed a different style of player to run the West Coast offense.

"The offense they had run at Nebraska was basically the offense that they had run for 40 years there," Norvell said. "It was an option-style attack. And one of the things, when you run the option, you have shorter linemen. They didn't have big tackles who could pass protect. So we had to recruit a certain style of lineman. We had to recruit backs who could not only run with the ball, but who could catch the football. We had to get wide receivers. A lot of the wide receivers they had were great blockers, but they weren't great pass receivers. And they weren't asked to run the way we asked them to run."

Callahan recruited Norman, Oklahoma, native Zac Taylor out of Butler County (Kansas) Community College as a fix at quarterback. Taylor originally had gone to Wake Forest and had only two years of eligibility remaining. He came in and started all 12 games in 2005 and posted more passing yards in a season (2,653 yards) than any previous Nebraska quarterback, besting Dave Humm's season record by nearly 600 yards.

Indeed the culture had changed. There were more than snowflakes flittering in the air in late November in Lincoln.

And in 2006 Taylor topped 3,000 yards passing and broke his seasonal record from 2005. In only two seasons he became the Cornhuskers' top career passer and had the top three passing games in Nebraska history and the top three total offensive games at the time.

"Zac Taylor really helped change it because he was the type of kid who could understand the passing game," Norvell said of the offense. "And he was a great leader and a great distributor of the ball, an accurate passer, and had tremendous field presence and management skills."

But as Taylor's career wound down, he could beat neither the Sooners (21–7) in the Big 12 title game nor Auburn (17–14) in the Cotton Bowl. As much as the win over Michigan in the Alamo Bowl had given hope to Cornhuskers fans the previous season, the loss to Auburn in the Cotton Bowl raised some questions, particularly about the man with the headset on the sideline—Callahan.

In the loss to Auburn, some of Callahan's play-calling came into question. With the game tied at 7–7, Callahan tried a fake punt early in the second quarter on fourth-and-one at the Nebraska 29. Auburn had gone absolutely nowhere on offense. The other score was set up by a Taylor interception. And this rather startling misplay set Auburn up for its only other touchdown of the game.

Also, late in the game it was difficult to tell just what Callahan was trying to do, trailing 17–14. He later said Nebraska was not in field-goal range at the Auburn 29, but it almost looked like the Cornhuskers were setting up for a field goal. Certainly, for all the razzle-dazzle of the West Coast offense, this was a fizzle of a series when one would have expected much more from Callahan, given his offensive credentials.

Nebraska drove to the Auburn 29. Callahan then called two mundane running plays, right up the middle and over right end, which hardly fooled the Auburn defense. The net result was, on third down, Nebraska was facing a third-and-nine. Callahan then tried a shovel pass, which lost two yards. So on fourth down and 11, when everybody in the Cotton Bowl expected it, Taylor finally got to limber up his arm. And with the defense expecting a pass, he predictably threw an incomplete one. Auburn got the ball back with 1:36 remaining in the game and basically ran out most of the clock.

That type of play-calling by Callahan looked more like Pop Warner than the NFL. Callahan had been openly critical of his play-calling in the loss to OU. But merely said, "We will look at that," when asked about his playing-calling in the Cotton Bowl.

After the game, Callahan said Nebraska was closing the gap on top 10 teams such as Auburn, Texas (another 2006 loss), and Oklahoma, but just wasn't there yet.

"We're getting there," Callahan said. "And I have a lot of confidence in this team as it grows and matures and goes into next season. I'm awfully confident that we will get better and we'll break through at some point. There's no question in my mind about that."

Unfortunately, for Callahan and the Cornhuskers nation, Nebraska would never crack the top 10 with him as coach.

And there were those past Nebraska players who were not completely sold on Callahan's West Coast offense.

"I don't have any problem with running or not running," said Mike Minter. "What I have a problem with is, if your offense is not teaching people to be physical, get off the ball and go. If your offense is about running sideways, you can't do that in college football. In the NFL you can do that because you have five linemen who can do that because they are all good. In college you can't do that, you have one or two maybe on that offensive line who are good. So you have to teach guys to be physical, get off the ball, knock people down. That was what Coach Osborne was all about."

A Total Defensive Collapse in 2007

With Arizona State transfer Sam Keller, a senior in the fold as the projected starting quarterback after Taylor's departure, Nebraska entered the 2007 season with hopes of a second straight Big 12

North Division title. The offense sputtered in a 20–17 victory at Wake Forest in game number two, and Nebraska was no match for powerhouse USC, 49–31, in game number three. The most revealing game in the early part of the season was the fourth game, a home victory over Ball State from the Mid-American Conference in which Nebraska's defense looked wretched in a 41–40 victory.

It was a precursor of things to come. Nebraska would give up more points in a season than any time in its history and also the most points in a game (76) to Kansas, a team the Cornhuskers used to dominate.

"I think they just quit playing for Kevin Cosgrove [the Nebraska defensive coordinator]," Taylor said. "I think they lost confidence in him. They lost trust in him. They lost their faith in him. They said all the right things to the media. But you don't give up 76 points, if you haven't lost something."

Still Nebraska, at 4–1, was in the top 25, when it played Missouri in Columbia. But Missouri, on the way to the most victories in school history (12), smothered number 25 Nebraska 41–6 and beat the Cornhuskers for a third-straight time in Columbia for the first time since the run in 1957, 1959, and 1961.

Things went downhill from there. Oklahoma State whipped Nebraska 45–14 the next Saturday in Lincoln at homecoming, when the 1997 national title team was honored. Much to the sideline horror of the 1997 national champions, the upstart Cowboys jumped on the Cornhuskers early and handed them their worst homecoming loss in 49 years.

The get-rid-of-Pederson-and-Callahan campaign was in full swing after this blowout.

And stories about the program were starting to circulate among the players, many of whom were on the sideline or in the stands for the Oklahoma State blowout. One fan held up the sign: "Surrender Steve Pederson."

"What happened is you got outside the family," Minter said. "You got outside of what made Nebraska special. And so when you come in and try and get rid of the walk-on program, you try to make it more of a professional thing. This is about family. You try to get rid of the guys who used to be there and paved the way. Before, they could come back any time they wanted to and come on the field and do whatever. I came back, and it was like Fort Knox. It became an institution as opposed to a family. I went to spring games, and you couldn't walk on the field unless you had a badge or something like that. It was crazy."

Taylor offered a similar story as to how All-Pro Will Shields from the Kansas City Chiefs was treated. He won the Outland Trophy in 1992 as a Cornhusker.

"Will Shields called up this past year," Taylor said. "He was getting honored. And he wanted tickets. Will Shields is my hero. He is my guy. He was told he would be given two free tickets. And if he needed any more, he could buy them. If I have a guy like Will Shields who has come from my program, I would bend over backwards for him. He hasn't been back in quite a while because he has been playing pro football. He is getting honored, and he only gets a ticket for him and his wife and he has to buy everybody else's tickets? It is not the fact that he can't afford them or anything. It is just not very nice."

Shortly after the Oklahoma State loss, Nebraska chancellor Harvey Perlman relieved Pederson, who had hired Callahan, of his duties and appointed former coach Tom Osborne as Nebraska's interim athletics director. Nebraska stood 4–3 with games remaining against Texas A&M, Texas, Kansas, Kansas State, and Colorado. Only a dramatic turnaround could save Callahan, with the athletics director who had hired him gone.

Osborne would make the decision on the future direction of the football program, whether Callahan would be retained or there would be a new head coach.

"People have a great deal of confidence in him," Chancellor Perlman said of Osborne. "But I hope people don't expect him to wave the magic wand."

Osborne, who said he was "mad" watching the Oklahoma State loss, added at the press conference, "We will give it our all the last five games and then sit down and talk after the season."

A decade after he had left the University of Nebraska to enter politics, Osborne said he "was surprised to be back in this venue." A major reason he was called back and would eventually pave the way for a new coach was that the defense hardly resembled what he had left. The 2007 Blackshirts looked like pinkshirts.

"Of the greatest concern to me was the defense, the ability to stop people," Osborne said later after he had fired Callahan. "As you know, occasionally you will win a game if you give up 50 points, but you are not going to win very many. So that was something that was a major concern."

Nebraska had allowed 40 points or more four times in a season for the first time in its first seven games, and 65- and 76-point defensive games were still to come after Osborne eye-balled Callahan up close. Osborne already began reaching out to former players.

"The first thing Tom Osborne did when he became interim AD, he sent a letter out to all the [former] players: 'I want you all back,'" Minter said. "'I don't know what happened before this, but I need you back.'"

The 76–39 loss to Kansas was an astounding number considering that in neither the 10-year periods of the 1970s nor 1980s, did Nebraska give up that many *total* points to KU. And a 65–51 loss to Colorado in the season finale left Nebraska with a 5–7 record, its second losing record in four years under Callahan. Since Osborne had taken over as interim athletics director, the Cornhuskers had beaten only Kansas State (73–31), and finished 2–6 and fifth in the Big 12 North Division. Callahan was fired after four seasons with a 27–22 overall record.

Taylor wonders if Callahan and, yes, incredibly Pederson, who is a Nebraska native, actually understood Nebraska, the state, the people, the school, and ultimately the football program and how it related to all of those entities.

"It makes me wonder if they ever understood it, quite honestly," Taylor said. "To me, it is a blue-collar, work-ethic type of state. It breeds loyalty, a lot of integrity and character. You heard Osborne mention that in a press conference. It is doing the right thing, even if you know you [could do the wrong] thing, and not get caught. It makes me wonder if Steve ever truly understood what Nebraska football was. What it meant to be the little guy in McCook, Nebraska, to the young kid who was running around in Wakefield, Nebraska, what it meant to the economy in Chadron, Nebraska. Whenever the Huskers lose, the state completely shuts down.

"Callahan has never rolled through these towns. Callahan spent four years here, and he would have no clue of how to get to Valentine, Nebraska. And Bob Devaney, Milt Tenopir (I'm not going to say Coach Osborne, but he knows how to get there), Charlie McBride, John Melton, and Dan Young—they could tell you every bar that is in Valentine. They can tell you all the players to come out of there. They could tell you the high schools, the high school coaches. If Callahan was asked that, he would have no clue. He had no clue of what the sense of community is. And it is outside that stadium. It goes all across that state."

Hiring Pelini Back to Nebraska

After eight days of his search, Osborne hired 40-year-old LSU assistant Bo Pelini, who had spent one season as a Nebraska assistant coach in 2003 and one game as Nebraska's interim head coach after Solich was fired. Pelini took the reins for the 2003 Alamo Bowl, and Nebraska belted Michigan State 17–3. He then left to become an assistant at Oklahoma.

Nebraska finished that 2003 season ranked first nationally in pass efficiency defense, second in scoring defense, and 11th in total defense. Nebraska had 47 takeaways and led the country in turnover margin. The following season, Pelini's OU defense was third nationally in points allowed. Each of the last three seasons, LSU has ranked third nationally in total defense under Pelini. Osborne liked Pelini because he has masterminded great defenses, possesses good leadership skills, and knows what makes Nebraska unique.

"His defensive credentials were outstanding everywhere he has been in recent years,"Osborne said. "He's a good communicator, a good teacher. It doesn't matter what you have in your head; if players don't understand it or can't translate it to the field, it's not going to make any difference. The second issue is leadership issues. I talked to an awful lot of players and coaches, and all of them are very impressed with his ability to inspire people, to get them to play with a lot of tenacity and emotion, and that's important. He has a good understanding of this state, with the importance of walk-ons, the importance of football to the state."

LSU's 2007 Outland Trophy winner, defensive tackle Glenn Dorsey, can attest to Pelini's intensity in the meeting room and practice.

"It doesn't matter if it is 5:00 in the morning, he is ready to roll," Dorsey said. "That's the biggest thing I like about him. He's always trying to motivate you and is making sure you are doing the right thing. You can talk to him about anything. And he's our general. He's our head guy. We just rally around him."

Pelini, from Youngstown, Ohio, was a standout free safety at Ohio State from 1987 to 1990, and as a senior won the most inspirational player award. After spending a season coaching at the University of Iowa and one in the high school ranks, he began a nine-year stay in the NFL, first as a scout and then assistant defensive secondary coach for the San Francisco 49ers under George Seifert, from 1993 to 1996. He moved to the New England Patriots as a linebackers coach under Pete Carroll for three seasons. And then went to the Green Bay Packers for three years in the same post for Mike Sherman before arriving at Nebraska in 2003 as defensive coordinator under Solich.

"What he has accomplished as coordinator is pretty remarkable," said Trev Alberts, former Cornhuskers All-American and CSTV analyst. "I remember when he got hired here the first time. He had been a linebacker coach for the Green Bay Packers. It took me about three games to say this guy knows what he is doing. It is the ability in the game to be able to make adjustments."

"I came here, and it gave me the first introduction to college coaching again, which was an adjustment after being in the pros for nine years," Pelini said. "Everybody knows what Frank [Solich] meant to this program. He was a great football coach and a great person. I learned a lot in that one year. One of the things I have learned is that you win with quality people. You win with high-character people and doing things the right way and not trying to cheat the system and trying to work with shortcuts. There are no shortcuts to success. You have to put in the work and establish a trust and do it together. Fortunately, I have been around the types of people and organizations that allow you to do that."

Pelini is expected to revitalize the walk-on program at Nebraska. He added, "One of the unique aspects of this job and the university is everything it means to the whole state. So the more young men and the more people and more towns you get involved and have represented on your football team and in your program around the state is going to keep building strengths."

Osborne, who has been retained as athletics director, has emphasized getting back to the grassroots.

"If you take the 1997 national championship team and you take a look at the offense for Nebraska, 10 of the 11 starters on offense were from Nebraska," said Aaron Taylor, who is from Wichita Falls, Texas. "I was the only out-of-state guy. When Osborne says we need to reconnect with these high schools and these players in the state, I am not saying it has to be that way because it most likely not going to be that way, maybe ever again. But these kids in the state, all they want to do is be a part of it. And if all they do is contribute during practice, that satisfies their need."

How much will Pelini change the offense?

"They've done a lot of good things on offense around here as of late," Pelini said. "They've been moving the football, so I don't expect any drastic, crazy, wholesale changes, but there will be some different wrinkles. Time will tell on that."

Callahan's offense was putting up good numbers. In his three career starts in 2007, Nebraska's junior quarterback Joe Ganz (after Keller was injured and lost for the season) registered three of the top five single-game passing performances in school history. And junior I-back Marlon Lucky was the first player in

Nebraska history to surpass 1,000 yards in career rushing and receiving.

Aaron Taylor believes the West Coast offense can work, if the right plays are called, harking back to the Auburn loss in the Cotton Bowl.

"It is still college football," Taylor said. "I don't care if you want to run the wing-T, if you want to run Osborne's old option offense, or Barry Switzer's old triple option. If you want to run a spread or a West Coast or whatever the hell it is, you still have to have the players for that system, and they will all work if you set up practice right. To me the West Coast offense can work if it is in Ann Arbor, Michigan, or Lincoln, Nebraska, or Austin, Texas—it can work if you have the right personnel and the right coaches coaching it. To me, I don't think people are upset with the West Coast offense. I think they are upset with the play calls in the West Coast offense—the lack of consistency and the lack of growth and the lack of understanding. And you are scoring 51 points, but you are giving up 72."

Mitner would like to see Nebraska in a spread offense such as the ones Missouri, Kansas, and Texas Tech run.

"Nebraska will get back to where it was because Tom Osborne is just that type of guy," Minter said. "He understands the game. He knows what is going on. Basically what has happened in the Big 12, and I think around college football, they have taken the option and moved it into the shotgun. They run the option out of the shotgun and they spread you out more, instead of keeping everything close and tight with the old option back in the day we were doing it. We just have to get after it. We can't run the West Coast offense in the Midwest. You see this trend."

Coming Over from LSU

Two days before he was to coach his last game for LSU against Ohio State for the national title, Pelini was dressed in black sweats with gold trim and a Tigers emblem on his chest. At Media Day at the Louisiana Superdome, Pelini answered more questions about

Nebraska than he did LSU: his contract, his staff, and Nebraska's de-recruits, those players who once said they were going to Nebraska but then changed their minds amid the chaos of recent months surrounding the Cornhuskers program.

To show the kind of person he is, he just couldn't leave LSU, just like he couldn't leave Nebraska in 2003, until the job was done. Aside from recruiting for Nebraska a couple of weeks, Pelini has focused on LSU's game defensive plan while filling his NU staff.

"I never really gave it a second thought," Pelini said the week before the game. "Coach [Les] Miles [the LSU head coach] never gave it a second thought. And I obviously had the support of Coach Osborne up in Nebraska. We've been through too much together. And I am committed to them, and we're committed to getting this thing finished and doing it the right way. And it would have felt like unfinished business."

Said LSU's All-American defensive back Craig Steltz, "We heard he had the opportunity to come back and coach for us, we were excited as can be. It is a dream come true for him to have a head-coaching job at Nebraska. But as a coach, you coach to play in the national championship, and as a player, you play to play in the national championship."

LSU beat Ohio State 38–24 in the Bowl Championship Series 1–2 game, and Pelini was headed to Nebraska with no second thoughts or forecasts of how good his defense will be in Lincoln.

"With the way college football has changed in the last decade," Pelini said, "I appreciate wins. A good defensive performance today is having one more point on the scoreboard. A lot of things have changed in college football, clock-wise and rule-wise.

"I had other opportunities to go other places, but I was not going to leave LSU unless the time was right," Pelini added, citing that he believed Nebraska was a "special place."

We'll soon see if he is a special coach for Nebraska.

sources

Broeg, Bob. *Ol' Mizzou: A Story of Missouri Football.* Huntsville, Alabama: Strode Publishers, 1974.

Cotton Bowl Media Guide, 2007.

Cotton Bowl Official Archives.

Dallas Morning News (1987–2007).

Duffey, Gene and Steve Richardson. *60 Years of the Outland Trophy,* Dallas, Texas: Atriad Press, 2006.

Fed Ex Orange Bowl Media Guide, 2005.

Fiesta Bowl Official Archives.

Fifth Down, Football Writers Association of America Newsletter, 1967–2007.

Kansas City Star (1978–1987).

McCallum, John D. *Big Eight Football.* New York: Charles Scribner's Sons, 1979.

Mizzou, Missouri Alumnus Magazine (Missouri Alumni Association Magazine) 1957–2007.

Official 2006, 2007 NCAA Division I-A and I-AA Football Records Book, Indianapolis, Indiana: The National Collegiate Athletic Association, 2006, 2007.

Shatel, Tom. *Red Zone: The Greatest Victories in the History of Nebraska Football.* Lenexa, Kansas: Addax Publishing Group, 1998.

Smith, Loran. *Fifty Years on the Fifty: The Orange Bowl Story.* Charlotte, North Carolina: Fast & McMillan Publishers, 1983.

Sporting News, August 27, 1984.

St. Louis Post-Dispatch (1960–2007).

Steele, Michael R. *Simply Devine: Memoirs of a Hall of Fame Coach.* Champaign, Illinois: Sports Publishing, 2000.

Sugar Bowl Media Guide, 2004.

University of Miami Media Guide, 2004.

University of Michigan Media Guide, 2003.

University of Oklahoma Football Media Guide, 2004.

University of Nebraska Football Media Guide, 2003, 2006, 2007.

University of Nebraska Official Athletic Website (www.huskers.com).

University of Notre Dame Football Media Guide, 2003.

University of Texas Sports Information Department Archives.